GREAT MYSTERIES

Custer's Last Stand

OPPOSING VIEWPOINTS®

Look for these and other exciting *Great Mysteries: Opposing Viewpoints* books:

GREAT MYSTERIES

Custer's Last Stand

OPPOSING VIEWPOINTS®

by Deborah Bachrach

Greenhaven Press, Inc.   P.O. Box 289009, San Diego, California 92198-9009

Library of Congress Cataloging-in-Publication Data

Bachrach, Deborah, 1943-
  Custer's last stand : opposing viewpoints / by Deborah Bachrach.
    p. cm. — (Great mysteries)
  Includes bibliographical references and index.
  ISBN 0-89908-077-4
  1. Little Big Horn, Battle of the, 1876. 2. Custer, George
Armstrong, 1839-1876. 3. Dakota Indians—Wars, 1876. I. Title.
II Series.
E83.876.B23 1990
973.8'2—dc20   90-36967
                                                            CIP

In loving memory of
"Uncle Sol"
Who adored a battle

Contents

Introduction

This book is written for the curious—those who want to explore the mysteries that are everywhere. To be human is to be constantly surrounded by wonderment. How do birds fly? Are ghosts real? Can animals and people communicate. Was King Arthur a real person or a myth? Why did Amelia Earhart disappear? Did history really happen the way we think it did? Where did the world come from? Where is it going?

Great Mysteries: Opposing Viewpoints books are intended to offer the reader an opportunity to explore some of the many mysteries that both trouble and intrigue us. For the span of each book, we want the reader to feel that he or she is a scientist investigating the extinction of the dinosaurs, an archaeologist searching for clues to the origin of the great Egyptian pyramids, a psychic detective testing the existence of ESP.

One thing all mysteries have in common is that there is no ready answer. Often there are *many* answers but none on which even the majority of authorities agrees. *Great Mysteries: Opposing Viewpoints* books introduce the intriguing views of the experts, allowing the reader to participate in their explorations, their theories, and their disagreements as they try to explain the mysteries of our world.

But most readers won't want to stop here. These *Great Mysteries: Opposing Viewpoints* aim to stimulate the reader's curiosity. Although truth is often impossible to discover, the search is fascinating. It is up to the reader to examine the evidence, to decide whether the answer is there—or to explore further.

"Penetrating so many secrets, we cease to believe in the unknowable. But there it sits nevertheless, calmly licking its chops."

H.L. Mencken, American essayist

Prologue

The Battle at the Little Big Horn

On June 25, 1876, many Americans were preparing for the country's centennial celebration, its one hundredth birthday party. In New York, Philadelphia, Boston, and Washington, red, white, and blue patriotic symbols fluttered in the breeze and decorated houses and shop fronts. The United States was strong, vibrant, and dynamic. As it began its second century, its people were filled with pride. They anticipated great things to come.

On that momentous day, far away from the nation's great cities, preparations of a different kind were taking place. In Indian territory, in what is now the state of Montana, clouds hovered in the summer skies. No breeze stirred the surface of the Little Big Horn River. But along its banks thousands of men, red and white, would go out to do battle and to meet their fates.

One of these men, a great Hunkpapa Sioux chief, had had visions of an enormous victory. His dreams of military glory had inspired his people. Another, a gallant American Civil War hero, had a reputation for leading fearless charges to victory. One of these leaders would not live to see another sunrise.

Opposite page: Custer and his men fight their last battle.

U.S. map showing the location of Custer's last stand.

In the East, the day ended in blissful ignorance of the battle. Even by telegraph, news traveled slowly a hundred years ago. But in the West, a tragedy of overwhelming proportions had taken place. George Armstrong Custer had led America's most famous cavalry unit, the Fighting Seventh Cavalry. They had clashed with the mighty Sioux nation led by Sitting Bull and Crazy Horse.

Custer and five companies of his regiment were totally destroyed. Only a horse, Comanche, badly wounded by bullets and arrows, survived the greatest defeat ever inflicted by Indians on an army of the United States.

Why Did It Happen?

How could such a disaster have happened? How could the greatest of Indian fighters, the hero of numerous Civil War actions, the youngest man ever to be named to the rank of general in all of American history, be destroyed in less than an hour? "Few events in American history," writes military historian Col. W. A. Graham, "have more profoundly shocked the American people or have caused more controversial discussion or debate."

Why Custer fought and lost the great battle remains a mystery. Curiously, a tremendous amount is known about the Battle of the Little Big Horn. Books, maps, paintings, and interviews with participants tell much about the great clash between red men and white men. Movies have filled our imaginations with that magnificent panorama of life and death on the American frontier during the Great Sioux War. But mysteries, as all good detectives know, can exist in the midst of a good deal of conflicting information.

Lieutenant Colonel Custer was known to the Indians as "Long Hair" because he customarily wore his yellow hair in long flowing curls. He prided himself on his hair, his long drooping mus-

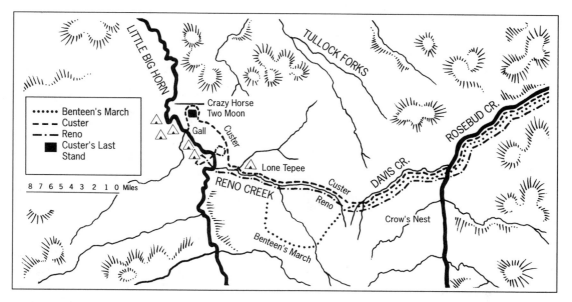

A map of the battlefield, showing the routes taken by Custer, Benteen, and Reno.

tache, and the elaborate uniforms he designed for himself.

Toward noon, on the last day of his life, Custer sat astride his favorite horse, Vic. He gazed down over the valley of the Little Big Horn River, looking for signs of the enemy. The fringes of his very unmilitary beige buckskin shirt fluttered slightly in the dry, hot air. He was lean and prepared, anticipating victory and glory.

Along the far banks of the twisting, winding river, were the Indians—the Sioux and their allies, the Northern Cheyenne and the Arapahoe. They were led by the fighting chiefs Gall and Crazy Horse and by the great medicine man, Sitting Bull. The Indians were determined to fight that day if they were forced to face their enemy. Custer, atop the hill, could not see the encampment with its hundreds of tepees. But he faced the greatest assembly of Indians ever to have converged in one place in North America.

The soldiers and their Indian scouts were nervous that hot summer day. They had been hunting the "hostile" Indians for weeks. Now, as the time for attack drew near, they were uncertain if their approach to the encampment had been detected.

Looking through his spyglass, Custer could see a few Indians tending their ponies. Some were hunting for wild turnips. They appeared to be unaware of the danger approaching. Custer believed he had caught the Indians by surprise.

But when Custer made his charge toward the village, his troops were met by overwhelming forces. The general, his two brothers, a nephew, and a brother-in-law were surrounded and destroyed. So too were the officers and men of the Fighting Seventh who had stood at Custer's side.

Bodies were stripped of all possessions. Many were scalped. A few were mutilated beyond recognition. The corpses of the Seventh Cavalry lay naked, rotting in the relentless summer heat. Two

Three of the victors at the Custer Battlefield cemetery.

days after the battle a relief column discovered them. Shocked troops were dazed by the enormity of the disaster and nearly overcome by the stench of rotting flesh. They dug hasty graves as their leaders tried to understand the events of the past few days.

A Great Mystery

Just how Custer met his death and who killed him will remain a mystery forever. Dead men tell no tales. When the war ended, whoever among the Indians killed Custer took that secret to his grave.

But many other mysteries also remain regarding the Battle of the Little Big Horn. Most important, how could it have happened? What role did Custer himself play in the unfolding of this most famous of American military disasters? Was there some flaw in his personality which led him to charge down those treacherous slopes toward a river and an enemy whose width and depth he did not know? Did Custer lack military ability, or was he guided by other than military considerations on that fateful day? Did those considerations lead him to disregard the orders of his superior officers? Was the famous general directly responsible for the death and mutilation of his men?

On the other hand, Custer's actions that day may have been entirely in line with accepted military traditions. He may have carried out with precision an action which was defeated by forces beyond his control. Perhaps the answer to the mystery of the battle's outcome lies in the behavior of his officers. Did they carry out their instructions to the best of their abilities? Were they loyal to Custer? Or were there other, angry, jealous impulses at work that stopped Maj. Marcus Reno and Capt. Frederick Benteen, Custer's two senior officers, from coming to the rescue of their embattled leader?

What of Custer's superiors? Gen. Alfred Terry was responsible for drawing up the battle plans that

"Long Hair" Custer wearing an unorthodox uniform he designed.

guided Custer's line of march. Custer had served under Generals Phil Sheridan and William Tecumseh Sherman during the Civil War. These men now directed the entire United States Army. These men knew Custer's character. They knew how he behaved in the face of danger.

What of Ulysses S. Grant, president of the United States? He was an old soldier who knew all about Custer's reputation for charging into the thick of the fray. The relationship between President Grant and his old cavalry subordinate in the Civil War may help to explain the outcome of the battle.

These men—Terry, Sherman, Sheridan, and Grant, generals all—were responsible for enforcing Indian policy. What role did these individuals play in the drama unfolding along the banks of the Little Big Horn River that sultry summer day?

The role of the Indians must also be considered. Why were the Indians concentrated in such a large group? Were they simply gathering fresh game as

An Indian artist, Amos Bad Heart Buffalo, painted this scene from the Custer battle.

was their custom during the summer months? Were they acting in defense of their treaty rights to land they had long held sacred? Or were they ruthless savages bent on destroying everything in their paths? Did the white people's attitude toward the Indians affect the outcome of the day's military action?

Questions Raised

Who knew, and who was supposed to know, the intentions of the Indians in the winter of 1875 and the spring of 1876? The government's agents on the reservations were obligated to report to Washington on the whereabouts of their charges. Did they do so? Was there enough information available to understand the intentions of the Indians and to help the army decide how to handle the situation? Or, more damaging still, were there individuals or groups who would benefit from a great and bloody clash out in the Indian territory? If so, is it possible that important news was deliberately withheld from those responsible for the safety of the army?

The deaths of Custer and his men raise these and other tantalizing questions. Answers can be found in the writings of hundreds of Custer lore enthusiasts. But not surprisingly, there are opposing viewpoints regarding all of the questions raised. The search for new perspectives is never ending and so the mystery continues. But even a partial solution to the Little Big Horn mystery must begin with a discussion of George Armstrong Custer. Ultimately, he was the man on the spot, the man who made the decision to charge to the Indian village. To begin to understand the battle, we must begin to understand the general who lost it.

"Instead of a thousand, the gallant 7th Cavalry encountered about five thousand Indians."

Elizabeth B. Custer, George Custer's wife, *Boots and Saddles*

"The fighting force of the entire village, under Sitting Bull and Crazy Horse, numbered nine hundred and fifty-six warriors."

Writer Fred M. Hans, *The Great Sioux Nation*

One

Was General Custer Responsible?

Did I hear the news from Custer?
Well, I reckon I did, old pard.
It came like a streak o'lightning,
And you bet, it hit me hard.
I ain't no hand to blubber,
And the briny ain't run for years,
But chalk me down for a lubber,
If I didn't shed regular tears.

The Poet Scout

George Armstrong Custer was born on December 5, 1839, in New Rumbley, Ohio. He was known as "Autie" by family and friends. Autie was an aggressive, assertive oldest son of a large farm family whose politics were Democratic. The sometimes dangerous pranks, games, and high spirits that marked his early youth followed him to West Point, the military academy. He graduated from West Point in 1862, the very last in his class. This was not because of lack of intelligence or imagination. It was lack of discipline that affected his work and the regard in which his teachers held him.

The dashing young army officer was nearly six feet tall. He was broad shouldered and athletic, and he was also a fine horseman.

The army had need of such men. The United States was engaged in a bloody civil war. A young, fearless cavalry officer who recognized no danger suited the needs of the Union army. In action after

Opposite page: Was the tragic fate of the Seventh Cavalry decided by the pride and ambition of this man?

Custer as a young Civil War officer astride his horse.

action, ignoring signals that would have warned away older, wiser officers, Custer led countless victorious cavalry charges. In many of these he showed a reckless disregard for his life as well as the lives of his men.

"Custer's Luck"

"Custer's Luck" became a byword for daring deeds on the field of battle which resulted in victory. He came to be a favorite of the great Union army leaders, Phil Sheridan and William Tecumseh Sherman. For his achievements he was promoted to the rank of brevet general, a rank gained temporarily on the field of battle. This rank would be reduced after the war to lieutenant colonel. Many brevet commissions were reduced after 1864. Once the war was over, there was no longer a great need for large numbers of senior officers.

Custer's brevet commission had been highly unusual. At the time of the wartime promotion Custer was only twenty-three years old. Never before or since has so young a man been made a general in the American army. Custer liked the title. Throughout the rest of his tragically short life, although officially only a lieutenant colonel, he was pleased to be known as "General Custer."

After the end of the Civil War, Custer still found plenty of excitement. He joined the newly formed Seventh Cavalry in 1866. As an officer in the "Fighting Seventh," George Armstrong Custer soon became the most famous Indian fighter in America.

Conflict Between the Settlers and the Indians

White settlers pushing westward came into conflict with the Plains Indians. The settlers wanted to farm the land or have their animals graze on it. They wanted to build towns and they needed railroads to take their produce to market. Many wanted to prospect for gold.

The Indians' lives depended on the plains remaining open, free for herds of millions of buffalo to roam on their seasonal migrations across North America. As the number of settlers increased, grazing lands for the buffalo began to disappear and the herds were endangered.

Tragic confrontations frequently took place between settlers and Indians. It was marked by fighting, burning, plunder, and murder on both sides.

The army was instructed to maintain law and order. Frequently the cavalry was called in to help the settlers. This terrible confrontation provided George Armstrong Custer with new opportunities for high adventure and for enhancing his reputation.

His exploits were described in newspapers across the country. He added to his own reputation through the many articles he sent to *Galaxy Magazine*. Custer's articles provided excitement to

Some Indians refused to leave their nomadic lives and continued to follow the herds of antelope and buffalo. This painting by Alfred Jacob Miller shows a "surround," where the Indians rounded up buffalo from the vast herds to use for clothing, shelter, weapons, food, and other needs.

young and old alike; they thrilled to the exploits of the famous Seventh Cavalry and its dynamic lieutenant colonel.

Conflict with the President

But suddenly, Custer's dreams seemed shattered. He found himself in a bitter political and personal conflict with Ulysses S. Grant, the president of the United States. Custer accused the president's brother of involvement in schemes to defraud both the army and Indians living on reservations. Custer—and others—said the president's brother was misappropriating high quality supplies paid for by the government and intended for distribution to the army and on the reservation.

In the spring of 1876 Custer was training the Seventh Cavalry for an expedition against the Sioux Indians. Suddenly he was ordered to appear before a congressional committee in Washington. Grant's political enemies wanted to question Custer regarding corruption in high places. Custer was to testify against Orvil Grant, the president's brother, and others. The president became so furious that he put Custer temporarily under arrest.

The president knew, however, that Custer was his best Indian fighter and that an expedition against the Sioux was to start in June. He soon ordered Custer's release, but Custer's position as commander of the 1876 expedition had been lost. Instead of being able to gain personal glory as the officer in charge, Custer would now have to serve under Gen. Alfred Terry.

General Terry had no experience as an Indian fighter. He was a lawyer. He was kindly and fatherly toward Custer. Terry admired Custer's military abilities and often sought the younger man's advice.

In early June these men led the Seventh Cavalry out of Fort Abraham Lincoln and off to battle. They were accompanied by the strains of a blaring army

General Terry liked Custer and respected his advice about Indian fighting.

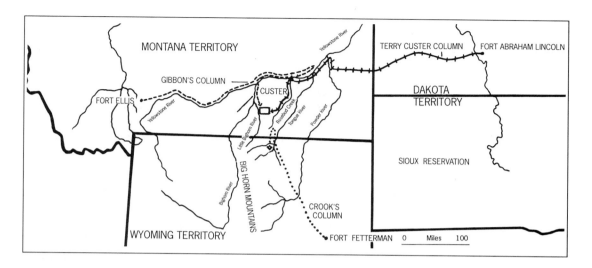

band, the bright flutter of flags, and the cheers of army wives waving their handkerchiefs, trying to hide their tears as their men rode off to war.

The Expedition of 1876

The 1876 expedition was the greatest military action ever undertaken by the government against the Indians of the Great Plains. General Terry's command was only one of three columns. The others were to come from Montana, under the leadership of Gen. Gibbon, and from Fort Fetterman in the south, under the leadership of Gen. Crook. Together these soldiers should have no trouble forcing the Indians back to the reservations. This would assure safety for the white settlers. Gold had been discovered in the Black Hills and prospectors were frantic to begin the search for sudden riches. In addition a railroad line was planned which would pass through Indian lands. Neither of these things could happen unless the Indians were subdued.

The Indians had refused to sell their sacred Black Hills to the United States government. Many were determined to defend with their lives land that

The Expedition of 1876 was to have been one of the army's most ambitious campaigns against the Indians. Army columns coming from three forts would converge on the Sioux and their allies and would either force them onto the reservations or destroy them. Crook's column was turned back by the Indians, Custer's column was massacred, and the Indians left the area. This meant Gibbons' column had no one to fight. This did not, however, stop the army and the settlers from seizing more of the Indians' land.

was crucial to the continuation of their religion and their way of life.

In December 1875, the United States government had ordered all the Sioux tribes back to the reservation that had been established for them. Those who refused to go there would be considered "hostile" and would be hunted down by the army. The Expedition of 1876, which led to the Great Sioux War of 1876, was designed to end all Indian interference with a white invasion of the Black Hills in what is now southeastern Montana.

As the confrontation began, America was watching. A great military victory over the "hostile" Indians would be the perfect culmination of the national festivities celebrating America's one hundredth birthday.

Instead, disaster struck. The "boy general," the darling of the press, the greatest American Indian fighter, the hero in buckskin, was destroyed. How could such a thing have happened? How could so fine a tactician as Custer have been defeated by untrained, undisciplined Plains Indians? Could the answer to the mystery lie somewhere in the personality of the man himself?

Custer the Ambitious

Certainly there are conflicting views of that unique personality. Col. Samuel D. Sturgis said that "Custer was a brave man, but he also was a very selfish man. . . . He was," wrote Sturgis, "insanely ambitious for glory." Sturgis, the actual colonel of the Seventh Cavalry, was temporarily serving in the South in 1876. He had good cause to speak against Custer. His own son had died in service with Custer.

Maj. James Brisbin of the Second Cavalry was also part of the 1876 expedition. He called Custer an "insufferable ass," a "wild man." And one of the enlisted men, Thomas Ewert, a private in the

James G. Sturgis died with Custer. He was the son of embittered Col. Samuel D. Sturgis who said that Custer was brave but selfish in his decision to fight the Indians alone.

Seventh Cavalry, wrote, "The honor of his country weighed lightly in the scale against the 'glorious' name of 'George A. Custer.' The hardships and danger to his men, as well as the probable loss of life were worthy of but little consideration when dim visions of an 'eagle' or even a 'star' [promotions] floated before the excited mind of our Lieut. Colonel."

The Role of Custer's Personality

Many historians have taken a hard look at Custer's personality for a clue to the unexpected defeat. In 1934 historian Frederic F. Van de Water wrote a book entitled *Glory-Hunter: A Life of General Custer*. In that book he wrote that Custer "followed Glory all his days. He was her life-long devotee. She gave him favor withheld from most men, and denied herself when his need of her was greatest." In addition, Van de Water believed that Custer was a very unpleasant man. He saw the cavalry officer as too self-confident, too strict in his discipline of his subordinates, and too disdainful of the weaknesses of his fellow men.

This negative view of Custer's personality is expressed still more vehemently by historian David Nevin in his book *The Old West—The Soldiers*. For Nevin, Custer was a "bad commander. Most of his men disliked him, distrusted him, feared him— and with good reason. He was personally undisciplined . . . [yet] to those who served under him he was a martinet, an extraordinarily strict disciplinarian. His ego was towering and demanded constant feeding."

The personality of Custer and its role in the defeat at the Little Big Horn has even interested psychiatrists. Dr. Charles K. Hofling wrote a book entitled *Custer and the Little Big Horn, A Psychobiographical Inquiry*. Dr. Hofling provides a description of Custer in which he suggests that the

"General George A. Custer was and will always be regarded as one of the most brilliant officers of the United States Army."

Editorial in the *Northwestern Christian Advocate*, September 7, 1904

"I have seen enough of Custer to convince me that he is a cold-blooded, untruthful and unprincipled man. He is universally despised by all the officers of his regiment."

Gen. David Stanley in a letter to his wife, 1874

soldier's behavior reached the point of continuous bragging. For Hofling, "Custer's ambitions—he wanted glory and reknown—were indeed strong." Hofling went so far as to write that Custer had a kind of personality disorder in which his feelings of self-importance influenced his behavior on the day of the battle.

Custer the Hero

But not all people viewed Custer negatively. Indeed, he had many admirers.

T. L. Rosser, for example, was a former major general in the Confederate army. Rosser wrote that he had "never met a more enterprising, gallant, or dangerous enemy during those four years of terrible war, or a more genial, whole-souled, chivalrous gentleman and friend in peace."

This was certainly high praise from a former Civil War foe. This view was echoed in the words

Custer leading his men into battle during the Civil War.

of Frederick Whittaker who, with the help of Custer's widow, wrote the first biography of George Armstrong Custer. In his book, *A Popular Life of General George A. Custer*, Whittaker called Custer "a great man, one of the few really great men that America has produced."

Charles Windolph served under Custer for several years. He wrote that Custer "died as he has lived—fighting his hardest at the head of his men."

Mark Kellogg was a *New York Herald* correspondent who accompanied the doomed expedition. He died by Custer's side at the Battle of the Little Big Horn. In one of his last dispatches to his newspaper, Kellogg described Custer as "a man respected and beloved by his followers, who would freely follow him into the jaws of hell."

Even the Indians had words of admiration for George Armstrong Custer. Low Dog, a Sioux Indian who had fought at the Battle of the Little Big Horn, said that Custer "was a brave warrior and died a brave man."

But perhaps the most moving testimonial to Custer's personality was provided by his wife, the former Elizabeth Bacon. She wrote that he was "the sunshine that lighted my life." Elizabeth Custer devoted almost sixty years of widowhood to preserving his memory.

The Campaign Plan

With such conflicting points of view, it is not easy to determine what role Custer's personality played in the fatal events of June 25, 1876. But perhaps some clues about the defeat can be unearthed by examining the campaign plans and the way in which Custer executed them.

Whether or not the thirty-six-year-old Custer liked the chain of command, Gen. Alfred Terry was in charge. He called together the main actors—himself, Custer, and Col. John Gibbon—for a

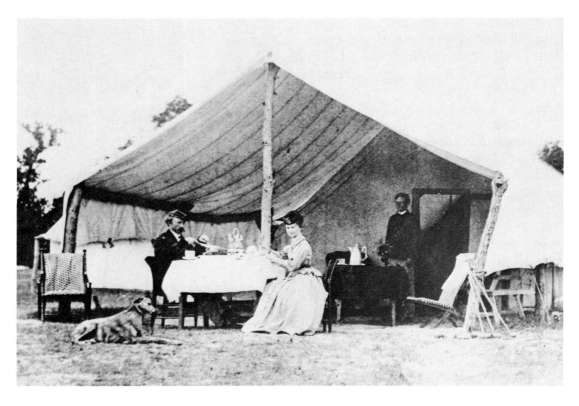

Custer's wife Elizabeth, or Libbie, joined him in the field whenever possible.

meeting aboard the boat the *Far West*. Terry developed a campaign plan. Each of these three men would lead troops to meet near the Little Big Horn River on June 26, 1876. A copy of the plan was handed to Custer.

Specifically, General Terry's orders to Custer described the areas in the river valleys where Custer would search for an Indian encampment. Custer's route was longer than the others because his cavalry could travel faster than the infantry, or foot soldiers, serving under Terry and Gibbon. If Custer found the Indians first, he was to send word to Terry who was following somewhat behind.

With some luck, all three commands would meet at the Little Big Horn River on the twenty-sixth of June and then take further action together.

The date of the intended meeting was quite clear. By that time they expected to find the "hostile" Indians who had refused to return to the reservation. The soldiers hoped to stop the Indians from escaping from their grasp as had happened so often in the past. The Seventh Cavalry believed that it could defeat the Indians in battle.

The Battle of the Little Big Horn took place on June 25, 1876, not on the twenty-sixth of the month. Custer's troops fought it alone. Custer did not send word back to General Terry that he had found the Indian encampment. He did not report that it was far larger than had been anticipated.

Did Custer directly disobey the orders of his commanding officer? Did he deliberately undertake an action in defiance of Terry who had called for joint efforts against the enemy? Or was battle inadvertently forced upon a reluctant officer who believed that he had no choice, that he had to fight on that hot afternoon?

Did Custer Disobey Orders?

Many believe that disobedience lies at the root of the mystery. Capt. William Ludlow served under General Terry. He wrote, "Custer crowed that he intended to 'cut loose' from Terry at the first opportunity and to run the campaign to suit himself."

Robert Newton was a cavalry officer who had once served under George Custer. He said, "after willfully disobeying positive and explicit orders, he [Custer] forced his luck against odds so great that had he survived he would have most likely been dismissed from the service by court-martial." And historian Frederic Van de Water concludes, "despite historical hair-splitting, there can be no doubt that Custer's superiors . . . regarded the plans they framed . . . as explicit and . . . mandatory."

Custer's supporters disagree with this position. Frederick Whittaker writes that Terry's plans were

"Thirsting for glory, Custer was accused of disobeying Terry's orders . . . and at the last moment dividing his forces in the face of a superior adversary."

Historian Robert M. Utley, *Custer Battlefield*

"While such tactics are not in accordance with the best teachings of the military art, nevertheless experience on the frontier had shown the advantage of attacking an Indian camp from several directions at the same time."

Historian Edgar I. Stewart, *Custer's Luck*

not specific but merely set "forth a guide to be followed . . . that the orders were entirely advisory and permissive." Therefore, "Custer cannot be held legally or morally responsible for any departure from Terry's orders, for the whole matter was left entirely to his discretion."

Capt. Robert C. Gartner, himself a veteran of the Indian wars, agrees. He writes, "Terry regarded his paper to Custer as instruction, not as orders." Gartner chides General Terry for any misunderstanding regarding the war plans. "With so much at stake as there was bound to be," writes Gartner, "he was too polite in his phrases."

The handsome, energetic, and ambitious young army officer, George A. Custer, as photographed by the famous Civil War photographer Matthew Brady.

Perhaps military historian Col. W. A. Graham provides the most even-handed treatment of the question of whether Custer disobeyed orders. He spent a lifetime collecting information regarding Custer and the Battle of the Little Big Horn. He wrote, "that Custer did disregard Terry's instructions seems reasonably clear; whether he was justified in doing so is a question which will bear examination."

Custer's Motive

And perhaps that question is the key to the mystery. Why did Custer fight the Battle of the Little Big Horn? Was he forced to or did he have a choice?

Frederic Van de Water does not believe that Custer had to fight the battle where and how he did.

Custer, the great Indian fighter, leading an attack on an Indian village in 1868, eight years before his last fight.

Van de Water wrote that for Custer, "There was a promise of glory in commanding this little army." He suggests that the decision to fight was bound up in Custer's recent nationally known dispute with the president over corruption in the handling of army supplies. The historian suggests that Custer fought the Battle of the Little Big Horn "to try to make up to President Grant through a victory over the Indians, . . . to ease the strain of his recent humiliations in Washington."

Gen. H. L. Scott was a young contemporary of General Custer. To him, also, the battle seemed unnecessary. He writes that George Armstrong Custer "could have led the main body of the Sioux into the agency [that is, back to the reservation], if he had not attacked first."

Historian David Nevin believes that something in Custer made it impossible for him to avoid battle. According to Nevin, Custer "wanted to be, once more, a spectacular war leader, to become great and famous. He himself explicitly described his craving to 'link my name not only to the present but to future generations.'" Such a man, Nevin believes, had to attack once the Indian village had been located. The details of the situation—the number of the enemy, the difficulty of the terrain—mattered little.

Did Custer Have a Choice?

Many, however, hold an entirely different view of their hero. Charles Windolph, the old trooper who fought on the day of Custer's death, certainly is one of those. Fifty years after the battle, Windolph told interviewers that Custer had no choice but to attack the Indian encampment. According to Windolph, Custer received information that led him to believe that the Indians knew the Seventh Cavalry was only a few miles away. Custer knew that if he did not attack, the Indians

would run away and he would be condemned for failure to carry out his instructions.

Historian Edgar I. Stewart spent many years collecting information regarding both the Indians' and the soldiers' views on the Expedition of 1876. In his book, *Custer's Luck,* Stewart suggests that Custer did not fight the battle to redeem himself. Stewart writes, "Custer's management of the affair would probably have been just about what it was had he had no difficulties with the President." Custer, Stewart explains, "regarded attack and victory as synonymous and his only concern seems to have been to keep the Indians where they were until he could strike them." Stewart quotes Custer's well-known boast that "There were not too many Indians on the whole North American continent for the Seventh Cavalry to handle."

"Long Hair Custer" certainly tried to carry out

A lithograph based on a painting by Cassilly Adams depicts the Indians routing the soldiers.

his boast. He knew from fresh tracks, recent animal droppings, and still-smoking fires that many Indians were near. He was so certain of victory that he conducted no reconnaissance. He did not study the river he must cross. He did not know the number of warriors he would face.

The general issued his orders. He divided his soldiers into four groups. Capt. Frederick Benteen and one group were sent off to the left of the village to keep the enemy from escaping. Capt. Thomas M. McDouglas and a second group were ordered to re-

A map of the battlefield drawn from the notes and sketches of a nineteenth-century soldier.

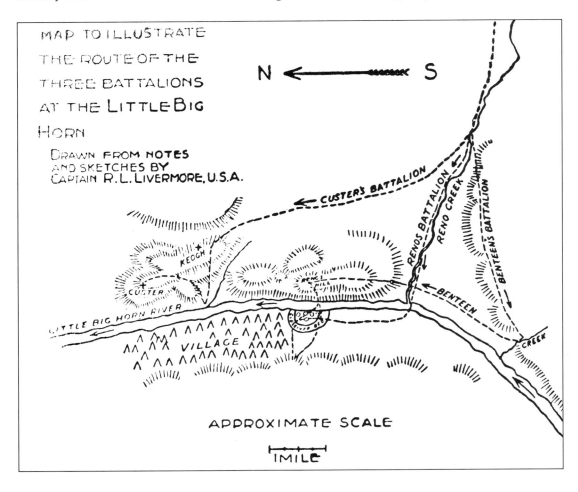

main with the pack train which carried the extra ammunition and supplies. Maj. Marcus Reno and his men were to attack the lower end of the village. Custer, with a total of 232 officers and men, would follow.

Why did Custer divide his troops? Would he have been victorious if he had led a unified cavalry charge? Is this the answer to the mystery of the loss of the battle?

Certainly bitter conflict raged and still rages over this question. In his formal report to General Sherman on the tragedy, Gen. Phil Sheridan wrote, "Had the Seventh Cavalry been kept together, it is my belief that it would have been able to handle the Indians . . . and that under any circumstances it could have at least defended itself; but separated as it was into three distinct [fighting] detachments, the Indians had the advantage, in addition to their overwhelming numbers."

It would appear that President Grant still bore anger against Custer, even in death. He wrote that he believed "Custer's massacre of troops was brought on by Custer himself, that it was wholly unnecessary."

Were Custer's Junior Officers at Fault?

Many historians support the president's view. Among them is Col. T. H. Coughlan. Coughlan wrote, "Almost his [Custer's] first act violated a cardinal military principle. He divided his inferior command into four factions." For Coughlan that is a major reason the battle was lost. Col. W. A. Graham agrees. He writes, "From the moment he divided the regiment and separated the various detachments so widely, without any plans for cooperation, what happened was bound to happen."

There is, however, another side to this matter. Frederick Whittaker defends Custer's approach to the battle as sound and time-honored. "Custer's

"Had Custer survived he probably would have faced a court-martial for disobedience of orders and incompetent leadership."

Historian Dee Brown, *The Year of the Century: 1876*

"That General Custer deliberately disobeyed Terry's orders I do not believe. Custer was intensely in earnest and fully determined to *find* the Indians and, when found, to attack them."

Historian Cyrus Brady, *Indian Fights and Fighters*

Custer and his men futilely shoot at hordes of Indians.

method," he writes, "was the one he used in the Civil War. He counted on the morale effect to be produced on an enemy by combined attacks and always found his calculations correct." In fact, Whittaker believes that only one thing could change the effectiveness of this approach. "This," he writes, "was cowardice or disability in the leader of any of the factions which were to work simultaneously, and this misfortune Custer had never hitherto suffered."

Whittaker's position was that the cause of the tragic loss was not due to failure on the part of the commanding officer but to shortcomings or worse on the part of his subordinates. This hint of failure or of darker doings among the junior officers is part of the legend that sprang up in the aftermath of the battle.

It is supported in the writings of men such as Lt.

Edward S. Godfrey who was at the Little Big Horn. Godfrey believes that Custer was defeated because of the overwhelming number of the enemy. However, he also pointed to the "incompetence of subordinates" as a major contributing factor.

Could this be the clue to solving the mystery of why Custer and the brave men who rode into battle with him were destroyed? Were the soldiers of the Seventh Cavalry killed and mutilated, some beyond recognition, because of the shortcomings of Custer's junior officers? Certainly the roles played by these men must be studied to understand the events of that day so long ago.

Two

Were Custer's Officers Responsible?

On the day that George Armstrong Custer died—shot through both head and heart—two other officers had combat commands along the Little Big Horn River. Both soldiers were Custer's senior in age but his junior in rank. One of these men was Maj. Marcus Reno. Reno led 112 officers and men into battle. Reno, like Custer, was a West Point graduate. Like Custer, he had served gallantly in the Civil War. As a result of his excellent record, Reno had been awarded the rank of brevet brigadier general of volunteers. After the war, that rank had been reduced to major.

Major Reno was dark and sleek in appearance. He had a thin mustache, a thin-lipped mouth, and "rather tired looking eyes." His men did not consider him to be a particularly pleasant person. He, in turn, did not think well of Custer. In fact, he had said that he "had small regard for Custer's military abilities."

Reno had had no experience as an Indian fighter. Nevertheless, because of Custer's temporary arrest by President Grant in the spring of 1876, Reno expected to lead the Seventh Cavalry in the

Opposite page: Custer and friends relaxing in front of the Custer home at Fort Abraham Lincoln. Custer and his wife are in the center.

Maj. Marcus A. Reno claimed to care little for Custer or his famed military abilities. Did Reno's jealousy and resentment lead to the tragedy at Little Big Horn?

summer campaign. Custer, however, returned to Fort Abraham Lincoln in the Dakota Territories, home of the regiment, in April.

Major Reno was now to be denied the long-hoped-for command position. Anger born of thwarted ambition was rife in the American army in the years following the Civil War. The army had been greatly reduced in size, and expectations for promotions were slim. Now, at the outset of a great campaign, Reno again would be a junior officer.

Until moments before the battle, Custer did not share his plans with Reno. About noon on June 25, Custer summoned Reno to his side. The Indian village lay before them. Most of it was hidden by a twist of the river. Custer said Reno would lead the action. Reno would cross the Little Big Horn River and attack the lower, or southern, end of the encampment. Reno understood that Custer would support him by following him into the fray.

Attack

With proud cavalry banners stirred into motion despite the hot, dry air, Reno and his men moved off at a gallop. They never reached the village. Instead, a wall of shrieking, painted Indians emerged suddenly from a screen of dust. Black Moon and some other Hunkpapa warriors had whipped their horses up and down in front of the soldiers, raising that dust screen to hide from view the women and children fleeing down the valley. Now many hundreds of Indian warriors began to charge the soldiers.

Major Reno ordered his troops to halt, dismount, and form a line of defense. Suddenly Reno's Indian scouts disappeared. His left flank was now totally exposed to the enemy bearing down upon him in very large numbers.

Reno ordered his men to fall back into a stand of timbers near the river they had just crossed. But

the Indians pressed their attack to the edge of the woods and into it, firing constantly at the now demoralized soldiers. Arrows and bullets found their targets even in the shelter of the trees. The soldiers were outnumbered by at least five to one.

The major believed his position was desperate. He looked back but saw no support coming from Custer. So he ordered his men to remount and retreat across the river and up the surrounding bluffs.

Retreat

That retreat became a nightmare. Not all the soldiers even heard the order. The Indians followed those who attempted to make their escape, hacking away at men and horses and taking many scalps. The Little Big Horn River ran red. The water was filled with dead and dying soldiers and their mounts. The survivors of the retreat scrambled desperately up the riverbank, exhausted and terrified.

What had happened? Why had Reno not carried out his orders to attack the village? Was the situation truly impossible and beyond his control? Was Reno a coward, or had the major, for personal reasons, deliberately undermined the entire plan set in

The Indian braves, creating a screen of dust around their encampment, allowed the women, children, and old people to escape.

motion by Custer?

Many people thought Reno should not have re-treated. He should have attacked the Indians and gone to Custer's aid. Frederick Whittaker condemns Reno bitterly for his actions on that day. Whittaker writes, "the failure of this movement, owing to his cowardice and disobedience, caused the defeat. . . . Had Custer's orders been obeyed, the troops would probably have defeated the Indians." Lieutenant Godfrey, himself a very young soldier that day, wrote later that Reno's behavior had been "cowardly and craven." Pvt. Robert S. Carter wrote that Reno's "entire conduct was that of a white-livered, yellow-streaked coward. He was terrorized and panic stricken and in a state of blue funk."

For Frederick Whittaker, it would have been better "if Reno could get no further [that] he should have defended himself . . . and died in his tracks, if need be, like a soldier." The words of Lt. Charles de Rudio in a backhanded way perhaps best express this view of Reno's behavior. De Rudio, who fought alongside Reno said, "If we had not been commanded by a coward we would all have been killed."

Reno's proposed route and his retreat.

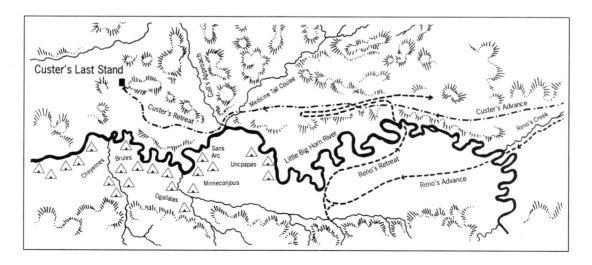

But Maj. Marcus Reno is not without defenders. Col. W. A. Graham wrote, "If Reno had rushed into the village, his little force would have been swallowed up and exterminated in five minutes." Historian David Humphrey Miller in his book, *Custer's Fall,* writes, "Reno could hardly have done better than he did in getting the remnant of his command to defensible positions on the bluff." Miller believes the reason there was a rush to condemn Reno was that the country was badly in need of a scapegoat to keep Custer's name clear.

Of what did Custer's name have to be cleared? Perhaps of failing to come to Reno's support. Years after the battle, Major Reno wrote, "I remember as I rode back to my command, the last remark I ever made to him was 'Let us keep together.' In his jaunty way he lifted his broad brimmed hat as much as to say 'I hear you.' But alas!, he did not heed me, and that afternoon he was cold in death's embrace." Reno spelled out his position very plainly. "If all our companies had been together," he said, "the Indians would have been driven from their village."

F. F. Girard, a civilian interpreter with the Seventh Cavalry, and Lt. George W. Wallace, among many others, have written that Major Reno rode with the promise of Custer's troops to follow his own. For these men, Custer's failure to support Reno led to the major's retreat from the village. These people believe that Reno's withdrawal was not caused by cowardice or disobedience or even a desire to get even with Custer. It was caused by Custer's failure to support his own men.

Reno's Hill

Major Reno and his surviving troops managed to claw their way to the top of what is now called Reno's hill. There they rested a short while. The wounded were cared for and weapons were reloaded. Then the small group of soldiers attempted

"Many today still believe that Reno permitted Custer to ride to his death, out of cowardice and hatred, and then, knowing that his commander was surrounded, withheld assistance."

Custer historian Bruce A. Rosenberg, *Custer and the Epic of Defeat*

"Major Reno was not a coward, as many believe. His career in the army during the Civil War and his promotion for gallant and meritorious services . . . are evidence of his courage."

Editorial from the *Northwestern Christian Advocate*, September 7, 1904

Reno's men frantically used barricades of dirt and the bodies of their own horses to protect themselves from the attacking Indians.

to leave the hill. They moved north, in the direction of recent gunfire and toward the place where George Armstrong Custer had last been seen alive.

Very quickly Reno and his men were driven back by many hundreds of Indians. So the troops retreated to Reno's hill. Using spoons and knives they tried to build defenses to protect themselves against the anticipated Indian attack. They used everything they had, including the dead carcasses of their once proud horses, as breastworks against bullets and arrows. Behind these defenses Reno and his men withstood repeated attacks until on June 27 they were rescued by General Terry and his men.

Could Reno Have Helped Custer?

Once Reno had reorganized his men, did he do all that he could to help General Custer? Could he have moved faster or been more deliberate in his attempts to find the general once he had escaped to Reno's hill?

Historian Edgar I. Stewart wrote, "Reno's retreat had the effect of releasing hundreds of Indians who then went up the valley to join in the attack on Custer." Thus, according to Stewart, "the effect of his actions on the subsequent fate of Custer was decisive." Historian James P. Murphy writes that for Reno on the hill, "there was every indication that Custer was heavily engaged and yet there was a total lack of support by Reno who thus violated one of the most elemental precepts of military science: in the absence of orders, march to the sound of the firing."

Historian and former soldier, Gen. James B. Fry agrees with this view. For Fry, "If Reno had marched [toward] the sound of the guns, it . . . might have enabled Custer to extricate the command."

Frederick Whittaker presents the case against Reno more strongly still. He suggests that for a long time after reaching the security of the hill, Reno continued to hear the sounds of battle to the north. Nevertheless, "he remained idle with this force while his superior officer was fighting against the whole force of the Indians."

A Court of Inquiry

This image of Reno deliberately letting his leader die is challenged by many people. In 1879, at Reno's request, a court of inquiry to review the events of June 25, 1876, was held at the Palmer House Hotel in Chicago. Many men present at the battle testified. At that inquiry, Gen. W. S. Edgerly told the assembly that it was generally believed that Custer and his men had "all been killed about half an hour after Custer's attempt against the north end of the village and that Reno had been on the hill only a short time before all firing ceased." Reno could not have saved Custer in the time available.

A photograph of "Reno's crossing" the year of the battle.

A court of inquiry decided that Reno was innocent of any wrongdoing in the death of Custer and the soldiers of the Seventh Cavalry.

Edgerly said that the evidence at the Court of Inquiry all pointed in that direction.

Edgerly also explained to the Court that no one on Reno's hill at the time of the battle had worried about Custer. They had believed that Custer had left them and gone to join General Terry.

The Court of Inquiry heard many statements, weighed all the evidence, and then reached its conclusion. The Court believed that Major Reno could not have come to the assistance of Custer. It held that all firing at the north end of the Indian village had ended before Reno could possibly have moved in that direction. Custer and his men had been killed in a very short battle.

Captain Benteen's Part

Col. W. A. Graham later reviewed all the evidence presented to the Court. He wrote, "Reno's battalion was in no condition to advance. He was short of ammunition and had many helpless wounded." Graham continued, "I hold no brief for Reno, but I believe in giving even the devil his due: and it is not necessary to attack and condemn Reno in order to account for what happened to Custer."

But Reno was not the only officer up on the hill. He was joined there by Capt. Frederick William

Opposite page: The "First Account of the Custer Massacre" as published in the Bismarck, Dakota Territory, *Tribune*, ten days after the battle.

Pierre, South Dakota

FIRST ACCOUNT OF THE CUSTER MASSACRE

TRIBUNE EXTRA

Price 25 Cents.

BISMARCK, D. T., JULY 6, 1876.

MASSACRED

GEN. CUSTER AND 261 MEN THE VICTIMS.

NO OFFICER OR MAN OF 5 COMPANIES LEFT TO TELL THE TALE.

3 Days Desperate Fighting by Maj. Reno and the Remainder of the Seventh.

Full Details of the Battle.

LIST OF KILLED AND WOUNDED

Bismarck Tribune's Special Correspondent Slain.

Squaws Mutilate and Rob Dead.

Victims Captured Alive, Tortured in Fiendish Manner.

What Will Congress Do About It

Shall This Be the Beginning of the End?

It will be remembered that the Bismarck Tribune sent a special correspondent with Gen. Terry, who was the only proffessional correspondent with the expedition. Kellogg's last words to the writer were: "We leave the Rosebud tomorrow and by the time this reaches you we will have

MET AND FOUGHT

the red devils, with what result remains to be seen. I go with Custer and will be at the death." How true! On the morning of the 22d Gen. Custer took up the line of march for the trail of the Indians, reported by Reno on the Rosebud. Gen. Terry, apprehending danger, urged Custer to take additional men, but Custer having full confidence in his men and in their ability to cope with the Indians in whatever force he might meet them,declined the proffered assistance and marched with his regiment alone. He was instructed to strike the trail of the Indians, to follow it until he discovered their position, and report by courier to Gen. Terry who would reach the mouth of the Little Horn by the evening of the 26th, when he would act in concert with Custer in the final wiping out. At four o'clock, the afternoon of the 24th, Custer scouts reported the location of a village recently deserted, whereupon Custer went into camp, marching again at 11 p. m., continuing the march until daylight when he again went into camp for coffee. Custer was then fifteen miles from the village located on the Little Horn, one of the branches of the Big Horn, twenty miles above its mouth, which could be seen from the top of the divide, and after lunch Gen. Custer pushed on. The Indians by this time had discovered his approach and soon were seen mounting in great haste, riding here and there, it was presumed in full retreat. This idea was strengthened by finding a freshly abandoned Indian camp with a [illegible] tepee, in which one of [illegible] had been left, about [illegible] the battle [illegible]

hand conflict with a dozen or more Siouxs, emptying several chambers of his revolver, each time bringing a red-skin before he was brought down—shot thru the heart. It was here Bloody Knife surrendered his spirit to the one who gave it, fighting the natural and heriditary foes of his tribe, as well as the foes of the whites.

The Sioux dashed up beside the soldiers in some instances knocking them from their horses and killing them at their pleasure. This was the case with Lt. McIntosh, who was unarmed except with a saber. He was pulled from his horse, tortured and finally murdered at the pleasure of the red-devils. It was here that Fred Girard was separated from the command and lay all night with the screeching fiends dealing death and destruction to his comrades within a few feet of him, and, but time will not permit us to relate the story, through some means succeeded in saving his fine black stallion in which he took so much pride. The ford was crossed, the summit of the bluffs, having, Col. Smith says, the steepest sides that he ever saw,ascended by a horse or mule reached, though the ascent was made under a galling fire.

Companies engaged in this affair were those of Captains Boylian, French and McIntosh. Col. Reno had gone ahead with these companies in obedience to the order of Gen. Custer, fighting most gallantly, driving back repeatedly the Indians who charged in their front, but the fire from the bluff being so galling, forced the movement heretofore alluded to. Signals were given and soon Benteen with the four companies in reserve came up in time to save Reno from the fate with which Custer about this time met. The Indians charged the hill time and again but were each time repulsed with heavy slaughter by its gallant defenders. Soon, however, they reached bluffs higher than those occupied by Reno; and opened a destructive fire from points beyond the reach of cavalry carbines. Nothing being heard from Gen. Custer, Col. Weir was ordered to push his command along the bank of the river in the direction he was supposed to be, but he was soon driven back, retiring with difficulty. About this time the Indians received strong reinforcements, and literally swarmed the hill sides and on the plains, coming so near at times that stones were thrown into the ranks of Col. Reno's command by those unarmed or out of amunition. Charge after charge in quick succession, the fight being sometimes almost hand to hand. But they drew off finally, taking to the hills and ravines. Col. Benteen charged a large party in a ravine, driving them from it in confusion. They evidently trusted their numbers and did not look for so bold a movement. They were within the range of the corral and wounded several packers, J. C. Wagoner, among the number, in the head, while many horses and mules were killed. Near 10 o'clock the fight closed, and the men worked all night strengthening their breastworks, using knives tin cups and plates, in place of spades and picks, taking up the fight again in the morning. In the afternoon of the second day the desire for water became almost intolerable. The wounded were begging piteously for it: the tongues of the men were swolen and their lips parched, and from [illegible] almost ex- [illegible] was

cept for the dead, Reno and his brave men felt that succor was nigh. Gen. Terry came in sight, and strong men wept upon each others necks, but no word was had from Custer. Hand shaking and congratulations were scarcely over when Lt. Bradley reported that he had found Custer dead, with one hundred and ninety cavalry men. Imagine the effect. Words cannot picture the feeling of these, his comrades and soldiers. Gen. Terry sought the spot and found it to be too true. Of those brave men who followed Custer, all perished; no one lives to tell the story of the battle. Those deployed as skirmshers, lay as they fell, shot down from every side, having been entirely surrounded in an open plain. The men in companies fell in platoons, and like those on the skirmish line, lay as they fell, with their officers behind them in their proper positions. Gen. Custer, who was shot through the head and body, seemed to have been among the last to fall, and around and near him lay the bodies of Col. Tom and Boston, his brothers, Col. Calhour, his brother-in-law, and his nephew young Reed, who insisted on accompaning the expedition for pleasure. Col. Cook and the members of the non-commissioned staff all dead—all stripped of clothing and many of them with bodies terribly mutilated. The squaws seem to have passed over the field and crushed the skulls of the wounded and dying with stones and clubs. The heads of some were severed from the body, the privates of some were cut off, while others bore traces of torture, arrows having been shot into their private parts while yet living or other means of torture adopted. The officers who fell are as follows: Gen. G. A. Custer, Cols. Geo. Yates, Miles Keough, James Calhoun, W. W. Cook, Capts. McIntosh, A. E. Smith, Lieutenants Riley, Critenden, Sturgis, Harrington, Hodgson, and Porter, Asst. Surgeon De Wolf. The only citisens killed were Boston Custer, Mr. Reed, Charles Reynolds, Isiah, the interperter from Ft. Rice and Mark Kellogg, the latter the Tribune correspondent. The body of Kellogg alone remained unstripped of clothing, and was not mutilated. Perhaps as they had learned to respect the Great Chief, Custer, and for that reason did not mutilate his remains, they had in like manner learned to respect this humble shover of the lead pencil and to that fact may be attributed this result. The wounded were sent to the rear some fourteen miles on horse litters striking the Far West sixty odd miles up the Big Horn which point they left on Monday at noon reaching Bismarck nine hundred miles distant at 10 p. m.

The burial of the dead was sad work but they were all decently interred. Many could not be reconized: among the latter class were some of the officers. This work being done the command wended its way back to the base where Gen. Terry, awaits supplies and approval of his plans for the future campaign.

The men are worn out with marching and fighting, and are almost wholly destitute of clothing.

The Indians numbered at least eighteen hundred lodges in their permanent camp, while those who fought Crook seems to have joined them, making their effective fighting force ne[illegible] and. These [illegible] carrying [illegible]

battle with Custer none are living—one Crow scout hid himself in the field, and witnessed and survived the battle. His story is plausable, and is accepted, but we have not the room for it now. The names of the wounded are as follows:

LIST OF WOUNDED

Private Davis Corey, Co. I, 7th Cav.right hip; Patrick McDonnall, D, left leg; Sergt. John Paul, H, back; Priv. Michael C. Madden, K, right leg; Wm. George, H, left side, died July 3d, at 4 a. m.; 1st Sergt. Wm. Heyn, A, left knee, Priv. John McVey, C, hips; Patrick Corcoran, K, right shoulder; Max Wilke, K, left foot; Alfred Whitaker, C, right elbow; Peter Thompson, C, right hand; Jacob Deal, A, face; J. H. Meyer, M, back; Roman Rutler, M, right shoulder; Daniel Newell, M, left thigh; J. Muller, H, right thigh; Elijah T. Shroude, A, right leg; Sergt. Patrick Carey, M, rigth hip; Privt. James E. Benett, C, body, died July 5th, at 3 o'clock; Francis Reeves, A, left side and body; James Wilbur, M, left leg; Jasper Marshall, L, left foot; Sergt. James T. Riley, E, back and left leg; Privt. John J. Phillips, H, face and both hands, Samuel Severn, H, both thighs; Frank Brunn, M, face and left thigh; Corp. Alex B. Bishop, H, right arm; Privt. Jas Foster, A, right arm; W. E. Harris, M, left breast; Chas. H. Bishop, H, right arm; Fred Homsted, A, left wrist; Sergt. Chas. White, M, right arm; Privt. Thos. P. Varner, M, right ear; Chas. Campbell, C, right shoulder; John Cooper, H, right elbow; John McGuire, C, right arm; Henry Black, H, right hand; Daniel McWilliams, H, right leg.

An Indian scout, name unknown, left off at Birthold; Sergt. M Riley, Co. I, 7th Infantry, left off at Buford, Consumption; Privt. David Ackison, Co. E, 7th cav., left off, July 4th, at Buford, Constipation.

The total number of killed was two hundred and sixty one; wounded 52. Thirty-eight of the wounded were brought down on the Far West; three of them died en route. The remainder are cared for at the field hospital.

De Rudio had a narrow escape, and his escape is attributed to the noise of the beavers, jumping into the river during the engagement. De Rudio followed them, got out of sight, and after hiding for twelve hours or more, finally reached the command in safety.

The body of Lt. Hodgson did not fall into the hands of the Indians; that of Lt. McIntosh did, and was badly mutilated. McIntosh, though a half-breed, was a gentleman of culture and esteemed by all who knew him. He leaves a family at Lincoln, as does Gen. Custer, Cols. Calhoun, Yates, Cook Smith, and Lt. Porter. The unhappy Mrs. Calhoun, loses a husband, three brothers and a nephew. Lt. Harrington also had a family, but no trace of his remains was found. We are indebted to Col. Smith for the following list of the dead; to Dr. Porter for the list of wounded, which is also full:

KILLED

Field and staff, George A. Custer Brevt. Major General.

W. W. Cook, Brevt. Lt-Colonel.

Lord Asst. Surgeon, J. M. DeWolf, Acting Asst. Surgeon.

A.C. Staff, W. W. Sharrow Surg-Major.

Henry Voss, Chief Insptr.

[illegible]

C, Allen, ---- Privt.
C, Criddle, ---- "
C, King, ---- "
C, Bucknell, ---- "
C, Eisman, ---- "
C, Engle, ---- "
C, Brightfield, ---- "
C, Fanand, ---- "
C, Griffin, ---- "
C, Hamel, ---- "
C, Hattisoll, ---- "
C, Kingsoutz, ---- "
C, Lewis, ---- "
C, Mayer, ---- "
C, Mayer, ---- "
C, Phillips, ---- "
C, Russell, ---- "
C, Rix, ---- "
C, Ranter, ---- "
C, Short, ---- "
C, Shea, ---- "
C, Shade, ---- "
C, Stuart, ---- "
C, St. John, ---- "
C, Thadius, ---- "
C, Van Allen, ---- "
C, Warren, ---- "
C, Windham, ---- "
C, Wright, ---- "
D, Vincent Charley Farrier
D, Patrick Golden, ---- Privt.
D, Edward Hansen, ---- "
E, A. E. Smith, ---- Brevt. Capt.
E, E. Sturgis, ---- 2d Lt.

The body of Lt. Sturgis was not found, but it is reasonably certain he was killed.

E, F. Hohmeyer, ---- 1st Sergt.
E, Egnen, ---- Sergt.
E, James, ---- "
E, Hagan, ---- Corp.
L, James Calhoun, ---- 1st Lt.
L, Miller, ---- Privt.
L, Tweed, ---- "
L, Veller, ---- "
L, Cashan, ---- "
L, Kiefer, ---- "
L, Andrews, ---- "
L, Crisfield, ---- "
L, Harrington ---- "
L, Haugge, ---- "
L, Kavaugh, ---- "
L, Lobering, ---- "
L, Mahoney, ---- "
L, Schmidt, ---- "
L, Lunon, ---- "
L, Semenson, ---- "
L, Riebold, ---- "
L, O'Connell, ---- "
L, J. J. Crittenden, ---- 20th Inf.
L, Butler, ---- 1st Sergt.
L, Warren, ---- "
L, Harrison, ---- Corpl.
L, Gilbert, ---- "
L, Walsh, ---- Teptr.
L, Adams, ---- Privt.
L, Assdely, ---- "
L, Burke, ---- "
L, Cheever, ---- "
L, McGue, ---- "
L, McCarthy, ---- "
L, Dugan, ---- "
L, Maxwell, ---- "
L, Scott, ---- "
L, Babcock, ---- "
L, Perkins, ---- "
L, Tarbox, ---- "
L, Dye, ---- "
L, Tessler, ---- "
L, Galvin, ---- "
L, Graham, ---- "
L, Hamilton, ---- "
L, Rodgers, ---- "
L, Snow, ---- "
L, Hughes, ---- "
K, D. Whitney, ---- 1st Sergt
K, Hughes ---- Sergt
K, J. J. Callahan ---- Corpl
K, Julius Helmer ---- Trptr
K, Eli U. T. Clair ---- Privt
I, M. W. Keogh ---- Col
I, J. E. Porter—the body of Lt. Porter was not found, but it is reasonably certain he was killed.
I, F. E. Varden ---- 1st Sergt
I, J. Burtard ---- "
I, John Wild ---- Corpl
I, G. C. [illegible] ---- "
I, S[illegible]

I, Henderson ----
I, Loddisson ----
I, O'Conner ----
I, Rood ----
I, Reese ----
I, Smith 1st ----
I, Smith 2nd ----
I, Smith 3rd ----
I, Stella ----
I, Stafford ----
I, Schoole ----
I, Smallwood ----
I, Tarr ----
I, Vaugant ----
I, Walker ----
I, Bragew ----
I, Knight ----
F, G. W. Yates ----
F, W. Van Rieley ----
F, Kenney ---- 1st
F, Nursey ----
F, Vickory ----
F, Wilkinson ----
F, Coleman ----
F, Freeman ----
F, Briody ----
F, Brandon ----
F, Manning ----
F, Atchison ----
F, Brown 1st ----
F, Brown 2nd ----
F, Bruce ----
F, Brady ----
F, Burnham ----
F, Cather ----
F, Carney ----
F, Dohman ----
F, Donnelly ----
F, Gardiner ----
F, Hammon ----
F, Kline ----
F, Krianth ----
F, Luman ----
F, Losse ----
F, Milton Jas ----
F, Madson ----
F, Monroe ----
F, Ruddew ----
F, Omeling ----
F, Sicfous ----
F, Sanders ----
F, Wanew ----
F, Way ----
F, Lerock ----
F, Kidey ----
F, E. C. Driscoll ----
F, D. C. Gillette ----
F, C. H. Gross ----
F, F. P. Holcomb ----
F, M. E. Horn ----
F, Adam Hitismer ----
F, P. Killey ----
F, Fred Lehman ----
F, Henry Lehman ----
F, A. Mclehargey ----
F, J. Mitchell ----
F, J. Noshaug ----
F, J. O'Bryan ----
F, J. Parker ----
F, F. J. Pitter ----
F, Geo. Post ----
F, Jas. Quinn ----
F, Wm. Reed ----
F, J. W. Rossberg ----
F, D. L. Lymons ----
F, J. E. Troy ----
F, Chas. Van Bra[illegible]
F, W. B. Whaley ----
G, Daniel McIntos[illegible]
G, Edward Botze[illegible]
G, M. Considine ----
G, Jas Martin ----
G, Otto Hageman ----
G, Benj. Wells ----
G, Henry Dose ----
G, Crawford Selby ----
G, Benj. F. Rodgers ----
G, Andrew J. Moore ----
G, Jno. J. McGinniss ----
G, Edward Stanley ----
G, Henry Seafferma[illegible]
G, John Papp ----
H, Geo Lee ----
H, Julian D. Jones ----
H, Thos. E. Mea[illegible]
M, Miles F. O'Hara[illegible]
M, Henry M. Sc[illegible]
M, Fred Stringe[illegible]
M, Henry Gordo[illegible]
M, H. Klotzbu[illegible]
M, G. Lawren[illegible]
[illegible] W. D. Me[illegible]
[illegible] Sm[illegible]

Capt. Frederick Benteen led one of the three arms of the Seventh Cavalry on the day of the fateful battle. Was Benteen's resentment of Custer at least partly to blame for the tragic outcome of the battle?

Benteen, Custer's other junior officer. The decision of whether to march toward the sound of the guns or to delay that advance was probably made jointly, and so Benteen's role in events must be considered.

Who was Frederick William Benteen and what impact did he have on the battle? Does his unique relationship to General Custer shed any light on the mystery of the outcome of the battle?

Like Custer and Reno, Benteen was a Civil War hero. He had been made a lieutenant colonel during the war. Like many others who remained in the army, he was reverted to his previous rank at its conclusion. He served in the Seventh Cavalry as a captain under Custer, although he was several years his senior in age.

Benteen was striking in his appearance. He had large, prominent eyes, a huge shock of prematurely white hair, and a very red face. All who knew him acknowledged him to be a very fine officer with nerves of steel in battle. He was also an excellent trainer of raw recruits.

Benteen's Hatred of Custer

Benteen's personality was as dramatic as his appearance. Those who admired him did so wholeheartedly. Those who did not felt equally strongly. Charles Windolph served under Benteen in 1876. Windolph later wrote, "I'm proud to have known and fought under Captain Benteen. . . . He was just about the finest soldier and the finest gentleman I ever knew. He was a wonderful officer." Gen. E. A. Garlington, who joined the Seventh after the battle, wrote that he "regarded him as a fine, practical field officer." And Gen. Hugh L. Scott noted that "Benteen was one of the most competent leaders he ever knew, a bluff and genial man when sober, a rancorous reviewer of old grudges when in liquor."

This other, rancorous side to Benteen's personality was noted by many. A *New York Herald* writer referred to this on July 11, 1876. "Benteen's dominant characteristic," the newspaper noted, "seems to have been jealousy and hostility to almost everybody and everything. There were few of his fellow officers for whom he had either liking or respect." The newspaper in particular noted Benteen's "hatred and jealousy of Custer."

Frederick Whittaker refers to Benteen's "malignant sneers" against the dead hero, expressed at the Reno Court of Inquiry in Chicago. The psychiatrist, Charles K. Hofling also notes Benteen's attitude toward Custer, which, he wrote, "seems to have reached the level of hatred."

Desertion Fuels Benteen's Hatred for Custer

Frederick Benteen made no secret of the raging hatred he bore for General Custer. He wrote after Custer's death, "I am only too proud to say that I despised him." Historian Frederic Van de Water suggests that for Benteen, "Injustice, real or fancied, to himself or another, rankled in Benteen's mind."

What is the injustice to which Van de Water refers? In an action against a Sioux Indian band in 1869 Custer had failed to rescue a certain Capt. Joel Elliott and nineteen other men. They had died horrible, slow deaths, their skin ripped from their bodies. They had later been found only two miles from the spot where Custer had spent his time destroying hundreds of captured Indian ponies instead of searching for the missing men.

Van de Water believed this episode filled Benteen with hatred for Custer. "A lifelong abhorrence [hatred], divinely consistent, had been well kindled in the bluff, white-haired captain before his chief left Elliott to his fate. There be no question that this desertion increased his hatred." According to Van de Water, "Benteen mourned Elliott with unpremeditated candour."

"Reno did exactly as he was ordered, by proceeding some 4$^{1}/_{2}$ miles and bringing the Indians to battle, in the valley, supposing all the while that Custer would be at his back support. In this Custer failed."

Indian historian Walter Camp, *Custer in '76*

"I am loathe to believe that Major Reno was a coward, but he certainly lost his head; and when he lost his head, he lost Custer. His indecision was pitiful."

Historian Cyrus Brady, *Indian Fights and Fighters*

Is this the key to understanding the battle? Is this hatred the reason Custer fought alone? What happened between these two men on June 25, 1876?

Custer summoned Benteen to his side and instructed him to take three troops of men, and go off to the far south of the Indian encampment. Custer told him to explore several valleys and to stop any Indians from escaping in a southerly direction through the rocky river valleys which lay to the south of the Little Big Horn River.

Benteen's Actions

Benteen rode off with his men. He had no knowledge of the specific orders given to Major Reno or how the battle was to be fought. He and his men rode for many miles but found no signs of the enemy south of the encampment. He decided that his had been a fool's mission, wheeled his troops around, and began to return to the place where he had last seen the remainder of the regiment.

As Benteen and his men, now tired and thirsty, picked their way over the rocky terrain, they were waved down by a non-English-speaking messenger from Custer whose name was Giovanni Martini. He could not tell Benteen what was taking place. Martini could only hand him a hastily scribbled note from General Custer. The note read, "Come on. Big Village. Be quick, bring packs!"

This meant trouble! Benteen spurred on his weary men and horses. He arrived at the river in time to see Reno and his frantic men off in the distance scrambling to get to the top of Reno's hill.

There Benteen joined Reno and helped the distraught major to tend to the wounded and to reorganize his demoralized troops. These tasks completed, Benteen and his men were part of the group which made the futile attempt to head north toward where they had last seen General Custer alive. But they

Custer's frantic note asking Benteen to bring help.

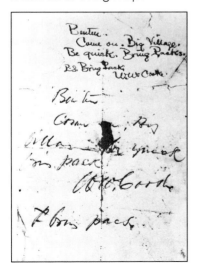

were driven back by warriors who had fought and killed General Custer. Benteen and Reno retreated to Reno's hill. There they were rescued two days later.

Could Benteen Have Saved Custer?

Did Benteen do all that he could to save his chief? Did he obey orders? Or did Benteen's hatred for Custer play a role in the terrible slaughter of over two hundred men of Custer's command? There are widely opposing points of view regarding the mystery of Captain Benteen's behavior that day.

Benteen himself placed all responsibility squarely on Custer's shoulders. He believes that just as Custer deserted Elliott in 1869, so too did he deliberately desert Reno. According to Benteen, "Custer promised to support Reno, then marched away, intending to attack from the far end of the village, the result of which was that all were killed." As far as Custer's orders to Benteen were concerned, the captain wrote that he believed that he was "being sent on a rather senseless errand, one possibly designed to keep him [Benteen] out of the battle." Charles Windolph referred to it as "valley hunting."

Historian Edgar I. Stewart writes that there was nothing that Frederick Benteen could have done to save Custer. Stewart believes that by the time the urgent note reached Benteen to hurry to help Custer, the general and his men were already dead. The actual slaughter of Custer and his men, according to Stewart, took less than an hour from start to finish.

Col. W. A. Graham concurs. Graham writes, "Benteen, who had no information of Custer's position or situation, could have accomplished less than nothing had he tried to cross the river and attack the village. He would probably have been cut to pieces long before he had reached the village." Once he was on Reno's hill, Graham believes, Benteen's

Trooper Charles Windolph admired Captain Benteen.

men and horses were far too exhausted from their useless errand to have gone to Custer's rescue. "Could Reno and Benteen together have done more? I think the answer is and must be 'No,'" writes Graham.

There are opposing views of the matter, however. Whittaker, for example, argues that Benteen "disobeyed orders." Benteen, according to Whittaker "was ordered to hurry to the battle. He obeyed by advancing three miles and there he joined Reno in a three-hour halt."

Did Benteen and Reno Fail Custer?

William O. Taylor was a private soldier in 1876. Years after the battle he described his view of Benteen's actions that fateful day: "Reno proved incompetent and Benteen showed his indifference—I will not use uglier words that have been in my mind—both failed Custer and he had to fight it out alone."

Charles Hofling takes this point of view one step further. For Hofling, Benteen was "certainly the dominant personality of the two officers on top of Reno's hill. He was seasoned in Indian warfare. He understood the order to go to Custer. Yet he did nothing, but placed himself under Reno's command."

For Hofling, "It seems clear that Reno was stalling and Benteen acquiesced. . . . This is not to say," according to Hofling, "that they knew or consciously suspected the desperateness of Custer's situation." But Hofling does believe that something caused both men "to behave in a fashion that was neither loyal nor gallant. One is led to the conclusion that their powerful negative feelings toward Custer caused them to . . . interpret the situation incorrectly and to rationalize their inaction."

Was Hofling correct or did Reno and Benteen truly believe that "not a soul in the command imagined that Custer was destroyed until General Terry came up" two days later? It can never be known for certain. In fact little is really known of the actual battle since there were no survivors of Custer's last stand.

It may well be that much of what happened that day was greatly affected by the interaction of angry men who held long grudges. But a larger question remains. Would anything have changed if they had cooperated better, if there had been a unified command? Does the mystery of the battle lie elsewhere, perhaps not with the soldiers but rather with the Indians who fought and won that day?

Three

Were the Indians a Superior Force?

When people discuss the Battle of the Little Big Horn, they generally talk about Custer and his loss or, worse yet, his massacre. They rarely praise the Indians or wonder about the victory that took place in that river valley in what is now southeastern Montana. In fact, it was the Indians' greatest victory in North America—and their last.

The northern Sioux tribes and their allies, the Cheyennes, fought the battle. Their camp was possibly the largest gathering of tribes ever to take place on the Great Plains. General Custer attacked it around noon on June 25, 1876.

On that sultry, summer day, the sun rose high in the sky over a great panorama of Indian life. Tepees and wickiups [these were small temporary brush shelters which could house one or two people] were arranged in seven great tribal circles on the flatlands along the Little Big Horn River. Behind the encampment, thousands of Indian ponies grazed on the rich green abundant grasslands. This was not a military encampment. Women, children, and old people were doing their daily chores when the soldiers of the Seventh Cavalry attacked.

Until 1876 the Plains Indians could live either as those did in the encampment or on reservations. On reservations Indians were taught to live as white Americans lived, "to walk the white man's road." The Indians on reservations no longer hunted for their sustenance. Instead they tilled the soil, went to school, and followed a sedentary life—that is, not moving from place to place.

Some Indians refused to live as reservation Indians. They chose instead to live the nomadic lives of their ancestors. Riding their wild ponies, they followed the herds of antelope and especially of *Pte*—the buffalo—across the Great Plains. This mobile source of food, clothing, shelter, glue, blankets, needles, and weapons provided everything the Plains Indians required. It was a symbol for their way of life.

Indians on the reservations were taught to give up their traditional ways and to live like the white settlers.

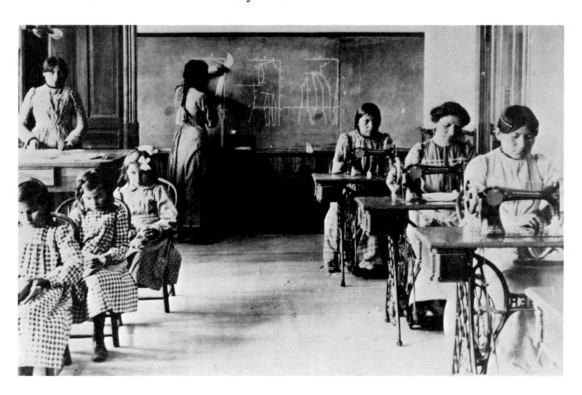

As the white settlers moved into Indian territory, conflict became more frequent.

Both the Indians and the buffalo had been pushed farther and farther west by white settlers, miners, soldiers, and railroad builders. These newcomers to the Great Plains threatened the existence of the buffalo herds and hence the nomadic Indian way of life. Here was a classic clash of two civilizations.

This process gained momentum in the years following the end of the Civil War. The period was marked by frequent bloody encounters. Many Indian villages were destroyed. Many isolated farm communities were burned. Railroad building crews were often in danger of attack.

The Government's Indian Policy

The government in Washington sent in the army to keep peace between the Indians and the white newcomers. There were many in government, particularly in the Indian Bureau, who believed that with good will and fair dealings, a just policy could be designed which would satisfy both sides. President Grant himself favored a policy of compromise.

But then rumors began to circulate in the western

towns that gold had been discovered on land set aside by the 1868 Treaty of Laramie for the Indians who did not want to live on reservations. Ironically, it was George Armstrong Custer who led an expedition into the Black Hills in 1874 and sent back the report that there was "gold in the roots of the grass." President Grant could now no longer hold back the tide of prospectors and others who urged him to change his Indian policy.

In December 1875, in clear violation of treaty rights, nomadic Indians were ordered to live on reservations. Those who refused were beyond the protection of the law. They were to be considered "hostiles" and would be tracked down by the army. For the army, the refusal of the Sioux Indians to come into the reservations was seen as an act of war.

Were the Indians in fact in a state of war with the United States government? Were they intending

A band of Sioux warriors photographed in 1898 by F. A. Rinehart. In the 1870s, groups like this were considered "hostiles" if they refused to stay on the government-run reservations.

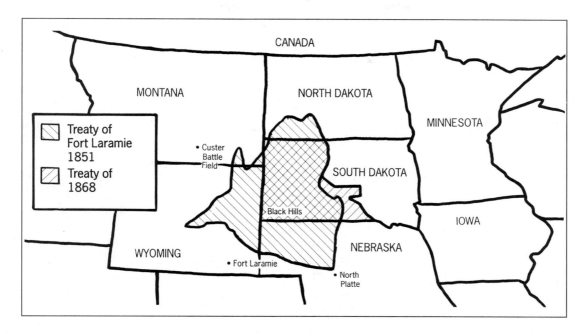

to launch a full-scale attack on the army and the western settlements?

According to historian Watson Parker, "The lack of food at the agencies [the offices which distributed food at the reservations] and the severity of the winter made compliance [with government orders] impossible." Thus, Parker writes, "regardless of their desires, the hunters were forced into hostility . . . [and] with the coming of the grass for their ponies in the spring of 1876, the Sioux, from hunt and reservation alike, took to the warpath in a desperate endeavor to secure in battle what they could no longer retain by submission" to the government.

Parker writes, however, that for many Indians in 1876 another force was at work. He states, "The proud, wronged, and warlike Indian was anxious for another opportunity for revenge." Historian Robert M. Utley argues the contrary. He believes the government forced war upon the Sioux nation. In his

Indian territory, as established by the 1868 Treaty of Laramie. This treaty reduced the amount of land reserved by an 1851 treaty. It was further reduced the year after Custer's death.

book, *The Indian Frontier of the American West 1846-1890,* Utley points out that the Indians had every right to roam the northern Great Plains. The Treaty of Laramie had been signed in 1868 between the United States government and the Sioux nation. It permitted those Indians who wished to do so to live forever "in that country north of the North Platte River and east of the summit of the Big Horn Mountains." To Utley, the reason the government came to consider the Indians hostile was easily explained by the discovery of gold in the Black Hills, the Indians' most sacred ground. Unfortunately, the gold fields were located on treaty territory. Utley argues that since the government could not control the greed of the miners and prospectors, it forced war on the Sioux nation. The Indians were out hunting buffalo and the soldiers went in search of them.

What Were the Indians' Intentions?

Historian David Humphrey Miller agrees that the Indians' intentions that summer of 1876 were entirely peaceable. Miller says that there was nothing unusual about the behavior of the Plains tribes; the Sioux had "always enjoyed visiting the old Sioux camping plain on the Little Big Horn." The place was ideal, according to Miller. "There was plenty of good water, lots of good grass for the pony herds, and plenty of wood. . . . It was a fine spot for fishing, or if the water ran high, for swimming." It was also a perfect spot for racing ponies, for rolling willow hoops, and for playing stick and hide games. The tribes had always journeyed to that place toward the end of June. Miller's book, *Custer's Fall*, paints an idyllic scene of summer peace disrupted by the deadly attack of the Seventh Cavalry.

For Miller, therefore, the Indians were victims of an unprovoked attack. "They were not rebelling against any authority they recognized at the time,

but simply exercising their age-old custom of following the buffalo herds northwest on the animals' annual migration."

Indians' Perspectives

In the years following the battle, many Indian participants were interviewed. Most of them also indicated that the Indians had not had hostile intentions. They were, in fact, surprised by Custer's attack.

Kill Eagle, a Sioux Warrior, participated in the great battle. He told an interviewer, "There was no design of a trap on the part of the Indians." They were surprised by the arrival of the Seventh Cavalry, according to Kill Eagle.

Crow King, another Sioux warrior, reported that his nation "did not want to fight. . . . Long Hair sent us word that he was coming to fight us and then we had to defend ourselves and our wives and children."

In 1877, the *Chicago Tribune* sent a reporter to interview Crazy Horse, one of the most important and famous Sioux. He told the reporter, "The attack was a surprise and totally unlooked for. . . . When

The encampment on the Little Big Horn was "a fine spot for racing ponies, for rolling willow hoops, and for playing stick and hide games."

Crow King said that the Indians had been forced into the fight with Custer.

Custer made his charge, the women, papooses, and children, and in fact all those who were not fighters, made a stampede in a northerly direction."

The army considered the Indians who lived off the reservation hostile. Many, including the Indians, believed that they were acting within the law. Nevertheless the Indians were prepared to fight if necessary.

Who led them? Is it possible that the presence of a great leader among the Sioux made a major contribution to the Indians' victory?

Unlike the process in the American army, the Plains Indians did not have a clearly defined chain of command that produced a leader. They had many chiefs. They followed these chiefs not because of their rank but because of the great deeds they had performed.

Sitting Bull

One of the greatest chiefs of the Sioux nation was Sitting Bull. Sitting Bull was a chief of the Hunkpapa Sioux Indians, one of the many branches of the great Sioux nation gathered on the bank of the Little Big Horn River.

He was a broad-faced, powerfully built survivor of many clashes with the American army and settlers on the frontier. He was advisor to his nation and a great medicine man, a kind of religious leader. For many years Sitting Bull had been a leader of those Indians who refused to sign formal treaties with the United States government. He lived on the plains as his ancestors had lived, refusing to adopt the white people's ways.

Several days before the great battle, Sitting Bull had participated in the annual great sun dance festival. He had performed a ritual prayer for advanced knowledge. He had prayed to *Wakan Tanka*, the Great Holy Spirit, who guided the Indians and who lived in the Black Hills.

Amos Bad Heart Buffalo depicts Chief Sitting Bull encouraging his braves to fight and win.

The medicine man had been rewarded with a vision. He foresaw that a great battle would take place. The vision showed many soldiers falling into the Indian camp. Sitting Bull interpreted this to mean that a great victory was forthcoming against the soldiers. The Sioux who fought knew about this vision.

Could Sitting Bull have so captured the imaginations of his people that he inspired them to victory? Certainly there are conflicting views regarding this great Indian leader. Gen. Phil Sheridan clearly was not intimidated by him. For Sheridan, there was "no real evidence that he was the leader of the hostile tribes." He believed that Sitting Bull's influence was rather slight, that he had done nothing to earn his reputation, "never having been anything more than an insignificant warrior with a few thieving followers."

Historian William S. McFeely presents a very different view of the Sioux medicine man. McFeely in his book, *Grant: A Biography*, depicts Sitting Bull as a statesman among his people. For McFeely, Sitting Bull clearly was distrustful of the government in Washington, and he convincingly conveyed his opinion to his nation. "That spring," writes the historian, "Sitting Bull began urging the Sioux to stand up against the white man."

Chief Sitting Bull. Was he more than a medicine man with an inspiring vision of victory?

David Miller elaborates on this theme. To Miller, Sitting Bull was a visionary and a healer, not just an ordinary medicine man. Miller saw Sitting Bull as a symbol of the old free way of life that the Indians held sacred but were losing quickly. "The example he set," argues Miller, "gave him dominion over the entire encampment."

Frederic Van de Water saw the Sioux chief as an "unreconstructed patriot who worked to keep inviolate [that is, sacred or unbroken] the land he roamed." Even Custer's most enthusiastic supporter, Frederick Whittaker, called Sitting Bull "an Indian of exceptional powers of mind whose stubborn heroism in defense of the last of his race was undeniable." An old Indian who in his youth had been with Sitting Bull at the Little Big Horn said he "had a big brain and a good one, a strong heart and a generous one."

Sitting Bull's Role in the Battle

Whatever his power to inspire, on the day of battle a leader must take his men into the heat of the action. What did Sitting Bull do on that great day of victory?

Sitting Bull may have inspired his people by the power of his vision. But his activities on June 25, 1876, continue to perplex people. There are conflicting accounts regarding his behavior at the moment the furious battle began.

Hump was a chief who took part in the battle. According to Hump, Sitting Bull personally led the attack that destroyed most of Major Reno's command and thus confounded all of Custer's plans. Then, Hump relates, Sitting Bull discovered that a second wave of soldiers was descending upon the village from the northern end. So Sitting Bull suddenly wheeled his warriors in a northerly direction and turned his long-building fury upon George Armstrong Custer.

Chief Hump with two of his wives. He participated in the battle at Little Big Horn and reported that Sitting Bull led the attack against Custer.

"Sitting Bull was a great chief—he had to be in order to maintain the position and respect that was his."

Historian Edgar I. Stewart, *Custer's Luck*

"You say you are no chief?"
"No!"
"Are you a head soldier?"
"I am nothing—neither a chief nor a soldier."

Interview with Sitting Bull, *New York Herald*, November 16, 1877

But Sitting Bull's biographer, Stanley Vestal, disagrees with the account provided by Chief Hump. In his book, entitled *Sitting Bull*, Vestal assigns an entirely different role to the great Sioux medicine man. According to Vestal's account, the Sioux chief did indeed play a major part in Reno's defeat but the attack on Custer was led by other warriors and chiefs. Vestal did not place Sitting Bull anywhere near the actual battle site where Custer's last stand took place.

Did Sitting Bull Fight?

A number of individuals, including James McLoughlan, the Hunkpapa Indian agent in the 1880s, argue that Sitting Bull played no role at all in the Sioux victory. They believe the medicine man went to the hills to protect the women and children and to make powerful medicine to help fulfill his dream of victory. One Sioux critic even expressed contempt for Sitting Bull. Low Dog told an interpreter, "If someone would lend him a heart, he would fight."

The *Saint Paul Pioneer Press* newspaper also participated in the attempt to determine what the great Sioux chief had done that day. It published its conclusion on July 18, 1876: "Sitting Bull had little or nothing to do with the fight. He was a medicine man of the Sioux and was in his lodge at the time making medicine for the destruction of the whites and the success of the reds."

Sitting Bull was unique among the Sioux leaders. His activities have attracted a wide variety of interpretations. Clearly his impact on the Indian victory has aroused discussion.

Yet even if his supporters are correct—that he was a great military leader—that still does not account for the strange events of that day. For even great leaders need able soldiers, and the Indians' record in fighting the white armies was not impressive.

Was there something that was different that day in the way that the Indians fought? Can the use of different tactics perhaps explain the perplexing events of that day?

Individually, the Indians of the Great Plains were ferocious warriors. They did not, however, follow specific leaders into battle unless the leader had demonstrated exceptional powers and skills. This was because the Indians saw battle in very individualistic terms. They tried to "count coups," that is, to count deeds of great bravery which they could later recount over the fire to the rest of the tribe.

The Indians were exceptionally skilled in the use of bows and arrows. They also carried knives, spears, and tomahawks into battle. In addition, they were learning the great power of firearms which some had acquired through trade or through battle.

Indian Warfare

In terms of battle tactics the Sioux were particular masters of decoy and deception. Many times in the past they had led soldiers into traps. They were highly skilled in this type of warfare since, ac-

Counting coups. To the Plains Indians, war was a game. A brave proved his worth by performing dangerous deeds. The Indians fought in a guerrilla style. Individuals would ambush, ride in for the attack, then whirl away to safety.

cording to historian Robert Utley, "the tactics used were merely an extension of the Indians' hunting skills."

General Sherman in his report to President Grant describes this kind of fighting. He wrote that "every canyon, every copse was a potential trap; every mountain, every mesa a watching post for Indian scouts."

The Indians were usually regarded as better, more fanatical individual fighters than the soldiers who were sent to defeat them. They were, after all, fighting on their own land. The soldiers, while having more formal discipline, were in enemy territory. Their homes and families were not in danger. In addition, one writer notes, the Indians had "an infuriating habit of slipping away without conclusive combat." Since the Plains Indians were among the best cavalry in world history, soldiers rarely kept up with them in a chase.

Soldiers' Tactics

But large-scale battle between Indians and soldiers seldom took place because the Indians almost never stood and fought a fixed action on an open battlefield, the preferred fighting style of the white armies. The Indians' traditional tactics ill-equipped them for success in such engagements. The soldiers, however, were trained to fight in fixed formations and were well disciplined under fire. Their training enabled them to win battles against overwhelming odds. When the Indians fought soldiers in fixed battle, the Indians almost always lost.

The Army of the United States expected the Indians to fight in their traditional manner during the Sioux War in 1876. General Custer clearly expected the Indians to fight as they had always fought. The campaign plans he received from General Terry called for dealing with fleeing Indians who would have to be rounded up and returned to the reservation. He sent Captain Benteen south of the Indian encampment to ensure that large numbers of Indians would not be able to run away in that direction.

A Special Fervor

What happened at the Battle of the Little Big Horn? Did the Indians use their traditional methods of warfare? If not, what methods did they use and why, and what effect did their tactics have on the course of the battle?

Gall, one of the important Sioux chiefs, reported that supernatural powers were at work on the side of the Indians. "Poor Custer, he could have saved his well-mounted command by flight but such a thought was no doubt farthest from his mind that day," Gall taunted after the battle. Gall believed that Custer could not win because "the Great Spirit was present riding over the field, mounted on a coal black pony and urging the braves on."

Some of the Indians described a special fervor that gripped the Sioux and urged them on to victory. Hump, one of the chiefs, describes the manner in which the Indians went into battle. "Thus our chiefs gave the 'Hi-yi-yi' yell, and all the Indians joined and they whipped each other's horses and they made such short work of killing them that no man would give an account of it."

Low Dog reported that he himself had urged his compatriots on to battle by telling them, "This is a good day to die; follow me." Then, he reports, "We massed our men, and that no man should fall back, every man whipped another man's horse and we rushed right upon them."

Crazy Horse reported that as the attack developed, the Indians did not run. Instead, they "divided their forces into two parts, one intercepting Custer . . . and the other getting in toward his rear." Then, outnumbering the soldiers as they did, the

Chief Gall believed that the Great Spirit fought on the side of the Indians on that fateful day at Little Big Horn.

Indians had "him at their mercy and the dreadful massacre ensued."

All these accounts suggest that something different from their usual fighting style had taken place. Dr. Charles A. Eastman, a military historian writing in 1900, suggested, "The simple truth is that Custer met the combined forces of the Indians which were greater than his own, and that he had not so much underestimated their numbers as their ability."

Survivors of the Seventh Cavalry who were fortunate enough not to have been with Custer that afternoon agreed with Eastman's conclusion. Lt. Edward Godfrey, attached to Reno's group, wrote that the Indians showed "unexpected cohesion." Unlike their usual battle style, they worked together

White Bird, an Indian artist, painted what he saw on the day of Custer's Last Stand.

as a unit. Reno himself reported that at no time did the Indians show any signs of fleeing. Captain Benteen agreed. He examined the battlefield two days after Custer's death. The stripped, mutilated bodies of the soldiers were found on the slope of a hill, in a manner defying all expectation. The evidence showed that the privates had been killed first. The officers' bodies were huddled around Custer. They were arranged in a manner suggesting that in the last moments of their lives they had rallied around their leader, as if to defend Custer to the death. In death, the corpses revealed that a unified, cohesive body of Indians must have overwhelmed and overrun the mighty Seventh Cavalry.

What gave the Indians the power to behave in battle that day as they had seldom behaved before? Was it possible that it was not a great spirit, or a wild desire for revenge which guided them and destroyed Custer? Was something even more deadly at work?

W. A. Graham thinks so. He believes that Custer and his command were destroyed because the Indians were better led, were more numerous, and had more and better firepower—guns!

Might the solution to the mystery of the great battle's outcome lie buried somewhere in the role played by weapons, either those in the hands of the Indians or those in the hands of the soldiers?

"I did not know anything about Reno's attack until his men were so close that the bullets went through the camp, and everything was in confusion."

Minneconju warrior Iron Thunder, quoted in *Bury My Heart at Wounded Knee*

"The Indians were not at all surprised at the appearance of Custer's command. They had known for some time—perhaps days—the approximate location of the regiment."

Historian Edgar I. Stewart, *Custer's Luck*

Four

Were Weapons the Key?

Along with strategy, tactics, and leadership, weapons are a key factor on the field of battle. New weapons often have altered the course of war, sometimes even the course of history. Early in World War I, for example, German machine guns stopped a massive, spirited French attack. What people thought would be a short campaign turned instead into five bloody years of war. During World War II the United States developed an atomic weapon. Four years of war against the Japanese ended within weeks of the dropping of this awesome new weapon on two Japanese cities.

Not only the twentieth century has seen rapid and major advances in weapons. In all ages important military changes have taken place. Many have suddenly and dramatically altered the balance of power between two enemies. The nineteenth century was no exception.

In the middle of the nineteenth century, weapons were undergoing very rapid developments. This was the great era of factory building. It was also a time of war. Thus the opportunity and the technology for the development of new weapons

Opposite Page: Were weapons the cause of the Indian victory and Custer's loss?

"We had seen for ourselves how admirably the Indians were equipped. We even saw a steamer touching at our landing its freight of Springfield rifles piled up on the decks *en route* for the Indians."

Elizabeth B. Custer, *Boots and Saddles*

"Although it has been alleged that the soldiers' carbines were outranged by the guns of the Indians, this has been denied."

Historian Edgar I. Stewart, *Custer's Luck*

came together. New and better guns were designed. These weapons became increasingly more accurate and could be fired at greater distances than in the past.

The old guns, like the flintlock smoothbore musket, could only fire three shots a minute. Because the gun was loaded through its muzzle, a soldier had to reload it from a standing position. These guns were only effective when a soldier got within one hundred yards of the enemy.

In the 1850s and 1860s, percussion rifle muskets became popular. They, too, could fire only three shots per minute. But because of the rifling in the muzzles—that is, grooves built into the gun barrels—these weapons were effective at 250 yards. Both the flintlock smoothbore muskets and the rifled muskets required ten separate motions to prepare them for refiring.

New, Superior Weapons

A major change in weapons occurred in the 1860s. The breech-loading cartridge rifle came on the scene. This was a superior weapon. A soldier could fire ten shots per minute against the enemy. His shots could now be effective at six hundred yards. Since the gun was a breech loader, a soldier could put in bullets and fire while lying down instead of standing up in the face of the enemy.

Guns played a very important role at the Battle of the Little Big Horn. Many participants referred to the presence of a good deal of firepower on both sides during that deadly action. We know that the government of President Grant sent out the army to hunt for hostile Indians and the campaign ended in tragedy for the army. Is it possible that weapons hold a key to the mystery of why Custer's command was destroyed? Could the Indians have possessed weapons, especially the newer ones, in such abundance and of such quality as to have overwhelmed the Seventh Cavalry by firepower?

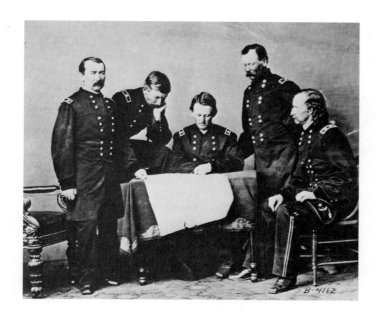

This Civil War photo shows Gen. Phil Sheridan (left) meeting with Custer (right) and other officers. General Sheridan claimed he would never have sent his troops into battle with the Indians had he suspected they had modern weapons.

These questions have been raised by many people and answered in a bewildering variety of ways. It is still not clear how well armed the forces fighting under Sitting Bull, Crazy Horse, and the other Indian leaders were on June 25, 1876. But the opposing viewpoints expressed may well help to understand the mysterious loss sustained by the army.

The Indians' Weapons

Some accounts state the Sioux really did not have a significant number of guns. This view suggests that Indians fought that battle in their old, traditional ways with their old traditional weapons —bows, arrows, spears, and knives. Historians Paul and Dorothy Gable believe this was the case. Their book, *Custer's Last Battle*, is a history based on many Indians' accounts of the battle. Red Hawk, the narrator, provides a moving, proud description of how the Indians fought against the soldiers.

"Our bowstrings twanged," Red Hawk recounts, "and flew like clouds of grasshoppers among their shadows, tumbling them from their

This lithograph of Custer's last battle shows Indians using both traditional weapons such as arrows and spears but also guns and rifles.

saddles." Then he provides a vivid description of how the Indians used tomahawks and knives to pull fleeing soldiers down into the river where the enraged warriors killed them.

Historian David Humphrey Miller also suggests that traditional Indian weapons were predominant at close to the moment of Custer's death. "Indians picked off Custer's men, one by one," Miller wrote, "mostly with bows and arrows. . . . A warrior thus armed could hug the ground to shoot without a sound or smoke to reveal his position to the enemy." This seems to explain for Miller why most soldiers who died with Custer were found lying

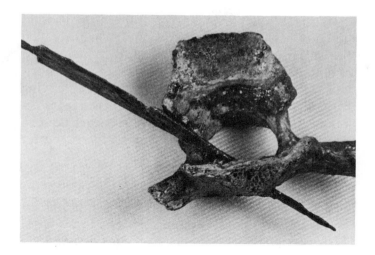

A relic from the Custer battlefield: a human vertebra pierced by a metal arrowhead.

face down. They had been shot in the back with arrows, not with modern weapons of warfare. (The bodies were all buried quickly, and no one recorded the kinds of wounds found.)

Clearly Gen. Phil Sheridan believed the Indians used traditional weapons. Sheridan had announced in 1875 that if he ever suspected that the Indians were receiving modern weapons he "would not expose our troops and trains to them but would withdraw our soldiers."

But others did not agree with Sheridan's assessment. The Indians themselves talked openly about what they had. After the war, Kill Eagle, a survivor of the battle, spoke of "all kinds of guns, Henry rifles, Winchesters, Sharps, Spencers." He said that many of the Indians had two or three revolvers apiece; all had knives and lances."

This sounds like an astonishing arsenal in the hands of the Sioux! Perhaps Kill Eagle exaggerated. But many others also noted the abundance of weapons in the hands of the Sioux that day. Sgt. Charles Windolph, who served with Captain Benteen, estimated that between 25 and 30 percent of all the Indians carried "modern repeating rifles."

Frederick Whittaker identified arms availability as the chief cause of Custer's death. He believes that the Indians would not have dared to wage war without possession of those arms.

Col. W. A. Graham spent many years studying the battle. From his investigations of participant accounts, the battle site, and army records, he also concluded that the Indians simply were better armed than the United States cavalry in 1876.

"Of late years," writes Graham, "a persistent effort has been made to minimize the armaments of the Indians at the Little Big Horn and to magnify the errors committed by the Seventh Cavalry." In his book, *The Custer Myth*, Graham dismisses this line of argu-

This drawing shows the Indians with both traditional and modern weapons.

Historian W. A. Graham states that many of the Indians pumped out shot after shot from their modern repeating rifles "held across the withers of their ponies."

ment. For him, "the claim now made in some quarters that only two or three warriors out of several hundred were possessed of repeating rifles seems somewhat absurd."

For example, Graham points out that "during Reno's retreat they swarmed along his flank, pumping shot after shot into his column from repeating rifles held across the withers of their ponies." Graham believes that guns, especially modern, efficient, rifled guns, destroyed the Seventh Cavalry.

The Army's Weapons

The question of what guns were available to the Sioux in 1876 is only half the mystery surrounding the role of weapons at the battle of the Little Big Horn. The second and equally important half is the matter of what equipment was available to the troops of the United States Army on the western frontier.

The army at this time was not held in high esteem. Its numbers had been cut dramatically following the Civil War. Many officers had been reverted to previous ranks because the government was trying to reduce expenditures. Recruits were often untrained. Many could not speak English. The low pay and poor

This photo shows part of Custer's expedition on the plains. Wagons carried supplies, and pack animals carried thousands of rounds of ammunition.

living conditions forced the army to recruit many poor immigrants who could find no other work. There were constant complaints regarding supplies of food, clothing, fuel, and, especially, weapons.

Were the Soldiers Well Armed?

Despite its shabby condition, the army was charged with many important tasks. It was supposed to keep miners out of the Indians' sacred Black Hills. It was supposed to protect settlers from warlike Indian bands. It was supposed to protect railroad workers who were extending the Northern Pacific railroad through land "permanently" given to the Indians.

Charged with these critical but somewhat contradictory roles, how was the army equipped to carry out its tasks? Despite the complaints, did the government at least supply its small army with the most advanced equipment? Or was the army's size a reflection of neglect in many other areas, including the crucial area of armaments? It is important to learn what types of guns and other equipment were available to the Seventh Cavalry in 1876. Therein may lie the missing key to the strange, otherwise unaccountable loss.

Sgt. Charles Windolph left modern readers a full picture of the arms available to the United States Army. Windolph reported that each trooper who fought at the Battle of the Little Big Horn had a single-shot Springfield 45-70, "an accurate and deadly weapon up to six hundred yards." In addition, Windolph stated that before the battle began each soldier had one hundred rounds of rifle ammunition and twenty-four of pistol ammunition. There were also additional supplies. Pack animals accompanying the troops carried thousands of rounds of ammunition for the rifles and pistols.

This account by a participant in the battle seems to suggest that the soldiers were very well armed. Charles K. Hofling uses this information to develop his viewpoint. He completely dismisses the notion that the soldiers lost the battle in 1876 because they were more poorly armed than the Sioux. Hofling writes, "It was natural enough for the army to seek to fix blame on factors other than those of strategy, tactics, and leadership" to explain the terrible events that befell the Seventh Cavalry. In Hofling's view, some Indians did have guns but they were in the minority and probably were not as skilled with them as were the soldiers. Hofling believed the question of arms was raised to avoid placing blame where it should rest—on the military leadership.

Faulty Equipment?

Having arms does not necessarily mean that they are the correct ones or that those available are in good working order. Sergeant Windolph described the equipment carried into battle by the Seventh Cavalry. Custer's troops appear to have been well armed. But

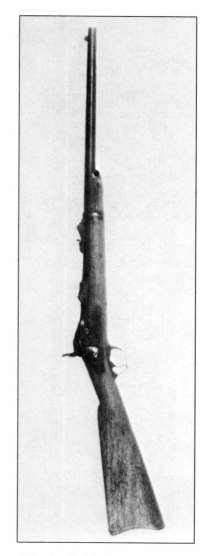

A Springfield single-shot carbine rifle, "an accurate and deadly weapon up to six hundred yards," according to Sgt. Charles Windolph. He said that each soldier at the Battle of Little Big Horn carried one of these.

Soldiers claimed that faulty weapons often blew up or jammed.

did those arms function properly? Many have investigated this aspect of the weapons question. Some have arrived at a viewpoint which differs greatly from Hofling's verdict on the role of equipment in the battle's outcome.

Charles de Rudio fought with Major Reno both during the initial attack on the Indian village and later on Reno's hill. During Reno's courtroom hearing in Chicago, de Rudio revealed what he knew about the arms available to the Seventh Cavalry. "I noted," said de Rudio, "that when the men on the line fired fast, they overheated their guns and had to use their knives to extract shells after firing eight or ten times."

One of de Rudio's comrades who survived the battle was Lt. Edward S. Godfrey. He had fought long and hard amid the carnage on Reno's hill. Godfrey testified at Major Reno's Court of Inquiry that one of the main reasons for Custer's defeat was the "defective extraction of the empty cartridge shells from the carbines [rifles]."

Edgar I. Stewart reviewed the evidence regarding army weapons and concurred in the view of many of the soldiers who had served in 1876. In his book, *Custer's Luck*, Stewart wrote that not only were the soldiers' weapons defective but the cartridges, which were made with copper casings, were too soft and therefore got stuck when fired repeatedly. He also wrote that "they were carried in leather belts and a chemical reaction occurred which made them difficult to extract in a carbine."

The Role of Larger Weapons

While some historians believe that defective guns contributed greatly to the defeat of Custer and explain the otherwise strange events, others clearly are not convinced that the mystery is so easily solved. They feel that factors other than small arms—pistols and rifles—played the critical role in the battle. What, for example, about larger arms—cannons and Gatling

Capt. Charles de Rudio, shown in 1885 with his two daughters. De Rudio reported that many of the soldiers' tools—weapons and ammunition—were faulty.

guns? Surely they were available to the army to use on this very important military campaign?

As has been noted, small arms were accurate at only relatively short distances in the mid-nineteenth century. Larger guns may not have been more accurate but their tremendous firepower could be deadly, especially in large concentrations. They could also be terrifying to an enemy who had never before witnessed their effects.

Larger guns with great firepower could also help reduce the impact of the size of a bigger opposing army. Certainly the forces fighting against Custer outnumbered the Seventh Cavalry many times over. Large weapons would have been useful.

One in particular, developed during the Civil War,

was available for use on the Great Plains during the Great Sioux War. It was called the Gatling gun, named after its inventor, Richard Jordan Gatling. Gatling had developed the first such weapon in 1861 and had patented his invention in 1862. The gun had seen use in the Civil War and then had been developed still further after the war by European powers because of its unique effectiveness against a massed enemy.

The Gatling gun was a crank-operated multibarrel machine gun. It was brought into battle on a two-wheeled wagon drawn by four horses. These were usually "condemned horses," that is, not fit for cavalry charges but clearly thought fit to be out on campaign. Once the gun was set up, a soldier turned its crank and

An old drawing of a Gatling gun on the wheeled wagon. If you look closely, you can see its multiple barrels.

the gun's many barrels spewed out bullets at a rate of 350 a minute!

The Gatling gun was little known to the Sioux Indians of the Great Plains. It was therefore something like a surprise weapon. If used properly, it could terrorize the enemy. It could make up for differences in the quality and quantity of weapons the opposing side could have put into the field. It could help halt an enemy charge. It might have made the Battle of the Little Big Horn the Seventh Cavalry's greatest victory.

Gatling guns were available to General Custer on the fateful night that he, General Terry, and Col. John Gibbon of the Second Cavalry made their final campaign plans. Maj. James S. Brisbin, serving under Colonel Gibbon, commanded a company of such guns. Twice, on the night before Custer left and on the morning of his final departure, Custer was offered the use of the guns. Each time he refused to take them on his march toward destiny.

Why Did Custer Refuse the Gatling Gun?

If the Indians were well armed but the army was still determined to drive the hostiles back to the reservation, why did Custer not take along a special and powerful weapon which could greatly assist him? Lt. Edward S. Godfrey wrote an account of a long talk Custer delivered to his officers on June 22 after he left General Terry's quarters for the last time. Godfrey reported Custer saying that he, Custer, "had declined the offer of the Gatling guns for the reason that they might hamper our movement of march at a critical moment, because of the inferior horses and the difficult terrain and because of the difficulty that they were pulled by condemned cavalry horses." Godfrey also reported that Custer cited as explanations "the nature of the country through which we would march." These marches, Custer estimated, could be as long as twenty-five or thirty miles a day.

In her memoirs of her life on the plains, Elizabeth

"The Springfield infantry carbine is a first-rate rifle, and probably the best that was ever placed in the hands of troops."

Col. John Gibbon, quoted in *Frontier Regulars*

"Custer's cavalrymen were practically disarmed because of the deficiency of that disgracefully faulty weapon [Springfield]. If they had been furnished with good Winchesters, or some other style of repeating arm, the result of the battle of the Little Big Horn might have been different."

Chicago Times war correspondent John F. Finerty, *War-Path and Bivouac*

Elizabeth Custer supported her husband during his ambitious life and she defended his reputation after his death.

Custer supported the decision made by her husband not to take along the guns. She wrote, "It was suggested that he should take a piece of artillery, but the scouts had described the bad lands over which they must march and General Custer knew that artillery would hamper his movements."

Ironically, Maj. Marcus Reno, later blamed by many for the tragedy, had supplied Custer with the justification for not taking along the Gatling guns. Reno had been out on patrol with the guns earlier in June. When he returned, he complained to Custer that the wagons on which the guns were mounted could not keep up with his reconnaissance. Reno had also suggested that the guns could not be moved easily enough to be used in an offensive action. He reported to Custer that they overheated when used continuously. This, he believed, caused the bullets to become jammed in the barrels.

Safety vs. Glory

These explanations of why Custer refused to take along the guns are disputed by some participants and historians. Some say it was more a question of personal glory. It was understood at the time that if the guns accompanied Custer, so too would Col. John Gibbon and perhaps Gen. Alfred Terry as well. Custer would have lost his independent command.

Late on the evening before the Seventh Cavalry left camp, Lt. J. H. Bradley wrote, "it is understood that if Custer arrives first he is at liberty to attack at once if he deems it prudent. We have little hope of being in on the death, as Custer will undoubtedly exert himself to the utmost to get there first and win all the laurels for himself and his regiment."

Frederic Van de Water agrees wholeheartedly with this point of view. For Van de Water, the "Glory Hunter," as he called Custer, had no intention of sharing the laurels of victory with any other officer on that campaign.

Charles K. Hofling enlarges upon this theme. In particular, he dismisses Custer's argument that the Gatling guns would hold up the line of march. Hofling reports a total of eighteen hundred horses and mules were available to the United States Army on its 1876 summer campaign. It would, therefore "have been a relatively easy matter to select sixteen such draft animals if Custer had wanted the Gatlings."

Hofling argues that the Gatling guns certainly were not a good offensive weapon, that is, to use when charging. They were, however, excellent for the defense, if the army was attacked by hostile forces. The obvious conclusion is that Custer had no thought of anything but the attack. He did not want to be slowed down either by cumbersome defensive weapons or by meddling superior officers. That his defensive firepower could have been increased by two-thirds if he

While the Indians used a guerrilla style of fighting, including ambush, the soldiers were used to fighting in fixed formations.

The soldiers' weapons were no match for the weapons or the spirit of the Indians on June 25, 1876.

had taken along the guns was no inducement to a man intent upon a spectacular offensive victory, according to Hofling.

What was it then, a justifiable reluctance to take along the powerful new weapons or a blunder made out of sheer desire for glory which led to Custer and his men being overwhelmed at their last stand?

The men of the Seventh Cavalry had been extremely well trained by George Armstrong Custer. For such men, under ordinary circumstances, difficulties with weapons or lack of Gatling guns might not have affected the outcome of the Sioux War. Certainly if battle conditions were overwhelmingly unfavorable on a particular day, the battle could have been fought at a later time.

That is what makes the Battle of the Little Big Horn such an extraordinary event. It was fought under strange circumstances in a year that was not an ordinary year. In Washington it was an election year. For agents on the reservations, it was a year of congressional investigations into their financial transactions. It was a year in which an enormous assembly of Indians was encamped along the banks of the Little Big Horn River. Some estimates put that number as high as fifteen thousand men, women, and children.

Nevertheless, the Seventh Cavalry sallied forth with every hope of victory. Was it possible that Custer did not know the size of the enemy forces facing him? Were there people or groups who wanted to conceal the information from him? Was there a massive breakdown in military intelligence which resulted in his death? More ominous still, were there people who might have benefited from the removal from the scene of such a charismatic character as the great Civil War hero? The answers to these questions may well lead to the core of the great, as yet unresolved, mystery of why General Custer and his men were slain.

"By turning a crank and feeding ammunition into a hopper, a Gatling crew could spew up to 350 rounds a minute from the bank of revolving barrels. Such fire power might have held the Indians at bay until help came."

Historian Robert M. Utley, *Custer Battlefield*

"Gatlings are worthless for Indian fighting. The range is no longer than the rifle and the bullets so small that you cannot tell where they strike."

Gen. Nelson Miles, quoted in *Frontier Regulars*

Five

Was Intelligence the Key?

There is an old saying that knowledge is power. For armies, knowledge about the enemy—its size, its armaments, its intentions—can be as important as the actual size or strength of one's own army.

This kind of knowledge is called intelligence. It is gathered by all means, fair and foul. It helps an army decide if it should make an attack against the front lines of an enemy. Sometimes intelligence indicates that an attack against the flank, or side of an enemy force, would be successful. There are times when intelligence provides ominous warnings that an army should retreat and fight another day—or be destroyed!

Occasionally armies have a good deal of intelligence but are unable to understand its significance. During World War II, for example, the secret Japanese diplomatic code had been broken by American intelligence experts by the summer of 1941. The United States knew a good deal about Japanese activities, even on Honolulu, Hawaii. Yet no one pieced together the scraps of information to discover that Pearl Harbor would be attacked in December of that year.

Opposite page: Custer (center) and four of his Indian scouts photographed during his 1873 Yellowstone expedition. Bloody Knife kneels on Custer's right. If Custer had followed the advice of his scouts, he would not have fought at Little Big Horn without first obtaining reinforcements.

"Custer was well aware that the nation gave the presidency to such men as Washington, Taylor, and Grant because they won her wars. Surely the man who ended the twenty years of Plains wars with the Indian would be no less rewarded."

Writer Mari Sundoz, *The Battle of the Little Big Horn*

"Anti-Custer writers have asserted that Custer was hopeful of a dark-horse nomination for president at the upcoming Democratic convention. . . . But there is no hard evidence for this."

Richard Slotkin, professor of American studies at Wesleyan University, *The Fatal Environment*

Sometimes leaders have only a few fragments of information but are able to cleverly take advantage of them. In World War II the Allies knew that Hitler feared George Patton above all other American generals. They used this knowledge to fool the Germans into believing that a massive troop landing would take place not in Normandy but elsewhere on the French coast.

Often leaders, either deliberately or through error, ignore the breathtaking insights that intelligence can provide. Occasionally these leaders gain glorious victories. More often, their followers are left to bury their fallen comrades' shattered remains.

At the time of the Sioux War in 1876, the use or perhaps the misuse of military intelligence may have played a dramatic role in the destiny of the Seventh Cavalry. The United States Army was relatively small given the task it was intended to perform. Information regarding the intention as well as the size of the Sioux tribes was vital for a successful campaign to force the Indians back onto the reservations.

Did anyone really know how many Indians were encamped along the banks of the Little Big Horn River? Who in the American army could judge the chances for victory? More frightening yet for the officers and men of the Seventh Cavalry, would anyone benefit from withholding available information or from overlooking its significance? The answers to these questions may help to explain how the unthinkable destruction of the Seventh Cavalry could have occurred.

Military Intelligence

In 1876 several individuals or groups of individuals had a direct interest in matters dealing with military intelligence—especially regarding the size and strength of the hostile forces which would face the Seventh Cavalry. Among these were the president of the United States, Ulysses S. Grant, the Bureau of Indian Affairs and its agents on the reservations, and George Armstrong Custer himself. All received information varying in amount and quality about what to expect during the expedition to the Great Plains. It is possible that the mystery of the Seventh Cavalry's defeat lies buried somewhere in the web of a deadly intelligence game played by these three somewhat antagonistic forces.

The President's Interest

President Grant had a good deal at stake when he settled the conflict between the prospectors and the Sioux Indians about mining for gold in the Black Hills in favor of the prospectors. The year 1876 was an election year and Grant wanted to serve a third time in office. A huge gold strike would help offset his administration's current economic problems and win him great popularity.

Grant needed to win this popularity. His administration was currently under attack for a variety of abuses. As one writer put it, "Disgrace and despair, like twin vultures, were hovering over his head."

It was Custer's misfortune to have contributed directly to Grant's problems. Custer was a friend of James Gordon Bennett, editor of the *New York Herald*, a Democratic newspaper, which opposed the reelection of the Republican Grant. Custer had sent to Bennett information which suggested that faulty goods were being sent to supply the army and that the profits were being pocketed by agents on the reservations and also by those close to the president.

In the spring of 1876 Grant's political enemies began to smell victory. A congressional committee ordered Custer to Washington to testify against the president's political cronies, especially Grant's dishonest brother, Orvil Grant.

The president's honesty was above reproach.

Ulysses S. Grant. Would he have sabotaged Custer's efforts against the Indians?

But he was intensely loyal to his brother and he was furious with Custer for having made public disclosure of Orvil Grant's schemes.

Grant angrily showed his displeasure by needlessly detaining Custer in Washington following his congressional testimony. Finally Custer left the city without permission. He was temporarily arrested when his train arrived in Chicago. But after intercession by Generals Sheridan and Terry, he was permitted to return to his troops.

Much had happened during the time Custer was absent from his command. In addition to being replaced as commander of the Expedition of 1876, he found that its start had been delayed from April until June. By then, hundreds, perhaps thousands of young Indian braves had slipped away from the reservation. Many of them were now armed with guns they had purchased from agents on the reservations or from traders who had come up the river.

As president, Grant was in a position to receive all intelligence from his officers. As a general and former leader of the Union army, he understood the significance of such information. Knowing what he knew, what were Grant's motives in sending Custer back to a delayed action against the Indians? Did he want a full-scale war in 1876, or did he merely want to act against the Indians who had left the reservation and thus gain control of the Black Hills? More ominous still, was he angry enough with Custer to deliberately try to deprive Custer of a victory?

The President's Motives

Historian William S. McFeely, in his book, *Grant: A Biography*, states that Grant could not have acted in a vicious, vindictive manner. He describes Grant as a humane man who favored kindness toward the Indians. He reports the president as saying that "as a young lieutenant, he had been much thrown among the Indians, and had seen the unjust treatment they had received at the hands of the white man." Such an individual would not willingly provoke a war which would result in the deaths of innocent men, women, and children.

Edgar I. Stewart disagrees with this point of view. He believes that the president was not concerned about the Indians' welfare, and that he deliberately created an impossible situation over the Black Hills to further his own political interests. Stewart writes, "It would not be the first nor the last time a national leader attempted to distract attention from domestic failure by the device of an outstanding military success."

Thus Stewart thought it was possible that Grant was using knowledge of what was happening in the Black Hills to bring about a war. Victory would bring national appreciation and perhaps a third term in office.

Grant and Custer

But did Grant want that war to succeed if he had to share the glory with Custer? Historian Dee Brown thinks so. After holding up Custer's departure for Fort Abraham Lincoln, Grant finally let him return to the Seventh Cavalry. "Perhaps," suggests Brown, "Grant himself was a victim of the Custer myth and believed with other Americans that the yellow-haired cavalry officer had special powers in fighting against the Indians." Brown does not think that knowledge of the size of the hostile force influenced Grant's decision. Brown believes politics, not intrigue, influenced the president's behavior.

Frederick Whittaker disagrees vehemently with this point of view. He believes Grant knew the size of the enemy force was growing quickly during the spring. Nevertheless Grant delayed Custer's departure to the war front. Why? According to Whittaker, Grant "was actually willing to imperil the whole fate of the Sioux campaign and to permit hundreds

"The Indians must have been assisted by racial renegades from white civilization. . . . including the philanthropists of the Indian Bureau, who had coddled and armed the savages."

Article in the *New York Herald*

"The army, professing ignorance of the increase in enemy strength, blamed the failure of the campaign on the Indian Bureau. . . . However, the army knew [via the Indian Bureau] that the young men of the Standing Rock Agency were heading west in large numbers."

Historian Robert M. Utley, *Frontier Regulars*

Gen. William Tecumseh Sherman denied that the government had information that would have saved Custer.

of lives to be lost, to gain his revenge on Custer." For Whittaker, Grant was an "implacable tyrant [one who could not be appeased], who was ready to forget his office, to prostitute his position, to sacrifice a hecatomb [a large scale slaughter] of innocent lives, to gratify his private revenge."

How could the president possibly achieve this terrible outcome? Perhaps by withholding intelligence reports of the alarming size of the enemy forces gathering along the edge of the Little Big Horn River.

In Washington, Gen. William Tecumseh Sherman, head of the army, denied that such information was available to President Grant. "Up to the moment of Custer's defeat," he wrote, "there was nothing official or private to justify an officer to expect that any detachment would encounter more than five to eight hundred warriors." Such a threat posed no danger to Custer and the Seventh Cavalry.

However, it appears that someone in high office knew that the Sioux nation had massed its forces. Somehow that information failed to reach the Seventh Cavalry before disaster struck. Col. W. A. Graham writes, "Such a warning from General Phil Sheridan via Fort Abraham Lincoln by courier was received a week after the battle, too late to avert disaster."

Was Crucial Information Withheld?

Is it possible that a conspiracy existed to prevent Custer from gaining a great victory? Edgar I. Stewart's words certainly are suggestive. He writes, "responsible government officers were not unaware that a concentration of hostiles was taking place."

Perhaps it is unfair to President Grant to accuse him too quickly of deliberately withholding military intelligence to satisfy a private vendetta against Custer. There were many extenuating circumstances. After all, in 1876 it was still difficult and dangerous to get information from the frontier to Washington. Information received had to be evaluated. The government then had to decide on a course of action and send back instructions to military leaders on the frontier.

The Knowledge of Indian Agents

But if not Grant and his immediate administration, who might benefit from Custer's defeat or at least from withholding important information? There are suspects, some far closer to the scene of the final tragedy than the aging American president. The Bureau of Indian Affairs in general and its agents of the reservations in particular knew a good deal in 1876. They were in an especially good position to be aware of the movement of Indian braves on and off the reservations. They also were directly or indirectly involved in weapons sales in the region.

The bureau and its agents were responsible for carrying out government policy and for providing food and other items for specific numbers of Indians who lived near the reservations. They were charged with maintaining the well-being of the Sioux, with educating them, with "civilizing" them. These men were in the best possible position to know in the spring of 1876 how many Indians were living on the reservations and how many had left to join the hostiles amassing around Sitting Bull.

Did the agents or their bureau have any reason to hide what they knew? Is it possible that important military intelligence was withheld, information which might have affected the entire campaign plans of the Seventh Cavalry?

The verdict is mixed on the relationship between the Indian Bureau and its agents and the Sioux Indians. Frederic Van de Water reports that within the bureau to which the fate of the Indians was entrusted there were many "men who broke their hearts in a vain effort to save their charges."

However, Robert M. Utley describes the entire system as involved "in corruption" with the agents "virtual despots accountable to Washington only in a vague way." Charles K. Hofling describes the outrageous prices charged for shoddy goods by the agents as a "serious evil," but one which was kept secret because the president's brother, Orvil Grant, was involved in the corruption.

In the view of Utley and Hofling the agents bought their jobs on the reservations with the intent of making fortunes by defrauding the Indians. They sold defective or rotten food and clothing at very high prices. Then they pocketed the difference and left the agencies after a year or two with huge fortunes, a portion of which they paid to Orvil Grant and his associates in Washington.

Historian David Nevin agrees with this point of view. He believes the rotten system affected soldiers

Indians on the White Earth Reservation in Minnesota are gathered for the issuance of flour rations by B.I.A. agents. Custer and others charged that the agents were corrupt, cheating both the Indians and the government.

and Indians alike. In his book, *The Old West: The Soldiers*, he writes that both were cheated by greedy, corrupt agents in order to make fortunes. The agents then funneled their profits back to Orvil Grant and to the Secretary of War, William W. Belknap, President Grant's longtime personal friend and wartime comrade.

Given this situation, would agents have any reason to falsify the number of Indians leaving the reservation in the winter and early spring of 1876? Yes, suggests Col. John Gibbon, because the agents themselves had forced peaceful Indians to leave the reservation. They drove them "to desperation by starvation and heartless fraud perpetrated on them."

Yes, suggests Edgar I. Stewart: "The agents made no reports because they made a profit selling supplies even for the absentees."

Yes, suggests Frederick Whittaker. He believes that "Sitting Bulls's truest and most persistent allies [in the battle against Custer] were the Indian Department and the Indian traders." They were concerned that the army would learn how much fine equipment had been sold to Indian warriors. Therefore they tried to conceal the nature of their business and the numbers of Indians who remained on the reservations.

Have we then finally arrived at the answer to the mystery of why Custer and the Seventh Cavalry were slaughtered? Was the great Indian fighter deliberately misled or denied intelligence, either by his government or by agents of the Indian Bureau? Could such intelligence have alerted him to the growing size of the Indian menace? Would Custer have changed his course if he had known what awaited him beyond that final hill?

Custer's Own Intelligence Sources

Before drawing this conclusion and closing the book on this mystery, wait! Custer was a great frontiersman. He was a scout with a great understanding of Indian tricks. He had insight into how the Sioux warrior thought.

It is possible that there were sources of intelligence available to him other than those provided through "official channels." Could Custer himself have been manipulating military intelligence to serve his own ends? What could such ends have been? The final twisted threads of this mystery may yet have to be unraveled to explain what happened at the Battle of the Little Big Horn.

The Seventh Cavalry marched out from Fort Abraham Lincoln to the rollicking strains of its marching song, "Gary Owen." Did General Custer have any direct notion of the size of the enemy force he was likely to encounter within the next several days? Did its size matter to him?

What Information Was Available to Custer?

Author Charles Kuhlman writes that as Custer approached the divide which led to the river, "There was absolutely nothing to warn Custer of the immediate proximity of several thousand belligerent Indians" except for reports from some of his scouts. These scouts began to tell Custer at this late date that the Sioux were "too many," a warning Custer refused to heed. Kuhlman, in his book, *Did Custer Disobey Orders?,* states that insufficient reliable intelligence was available to Custer as he planned and then prepared to carry out the Expedition of 1876.

Maj. Marcus Reno refers to available information from a different perspective. Reno told his own military tribunal in Chicago in 1877, "Our greatest mistake from the first was that we underestimated the strength of the Indians and it was this alone which led to such disastrous results." This account suggests faulty use of available information.

Lt. Edward S. Godfrey wrote many years after the battle that Indians from the Missouri Region and Nebraska had come to join Sitting Bull.

Edward S. Godfrey thought Custer would have received important information from the Indian agents if many Indians had left the reservations to join Sitting Bull and the other "hostiles" at the Little Big Horn.

However, according to Godfrey, Custer expected that if that were to occur, he would have been given ample warning by the agents of the Bureau of Indian Affairs or the Indian Department.

In 1896 Gen. James B. Fry wrote, "Believing as Custer and his superiors did, that his six hundred troopers were opposed by only five hundred or at most eight hundred warriors, his attack showed neither desperation or rashness."

Both Godfrey and Fry believed a lack of sufficient military intelligence, not deliberate misuse of available information, determined the outcome of the bloody battle.

Was Custer Forewarned?

Other writers, however, suggest that information was neither withheld nor falsified. Historian Jane Stewart wrote a long introduction to Elizabeth Custer's account of her life on the Great Plains. Stewart believes that there could have been little doubt in Custer's mind regarding the size of the force he was pursuing. "The number of Indians," she explains, "can be estimated by following the trail far enough to get its average width and the size of the circle grazed over at night by the ponies on which the warriors ride." It is Jane Stewart's view that days before the battle, Custer knew he would have to fight a formidable enemy, far larger than his own regiment.

Sgt. Charles Windolph reported, "Apparently the Indian scouts, especially the old guides, knew that there were several thousands of the hostiles, but it is my impression that Custer and most of the officers thought they'd have to whip somewhere between a thousand and fifteen hundred." This account also suggests that Custer had military intelligence available to him in advance of the battle which might have made him alter his plans.

W. A. Graham interviewed many Indian scout

"On June 25, 1876 the nation was shocked by the great disaster in Montana, the complete massacre of General Custer and his men."

Outstanding Historical Events [from a preface to the book, no author cited]

"Strictly speaking the destruction of General Custer's command was not a massacre, since it involved only soldiers fighting in open battle."

Chicago Times war correspondent John F. Finerty, *War-Path and Bivouac*

Indian scout Bloody Knife, Custer, and two other soldiers, posed with a bear they shot.

survivors of the battle. Their stories provide additional clues to the solution of the mystery. White-Man-Runs-Him noted, "We scouts thought that there were too many Indians for Custer to fight." He added, "I would say there were between four and five thousand warriors. It was the biggest Indian camp I had ever seen." Bloody Knife, another scout, "bade farewell to the sun in sign language, saying 'I shall not see you go down behind the hills tonight.'" Bloody Knife was shot in the opening movements of the battle in which Major Reno was forced to retreat.

Graham reports that Goes Ahead added funeral feathers to his hair and that White-Man-Runs-Him painted sacred white clay on his face. These were all signs of preparation for death, traditional to the

Arakara scouts who accompanied the doomed Seventh Cavalry.

David Humphrey Miller also recorded Indian impressions of the time before the attack. General Custer witnessed the scouts' death preparations. According to Miller, when the general saw these well-understood signs, "Custer's face drained of color and then he strode away." He did not, however, await reinforcements.

All of this suggests that Custer had available a good deal of intelligence. He knew by the evening of the twenty-fourth of June that the Sioux were close to his forces. By the contours of the fresh pony trail, he could guess the size of those forces. Custer was vastly outnumbered. General Terry and

Custer scout White-Man-Runs-Him and former Lt. Edward S. Godfrey participate in a ceremony on the fiftieth anniversary of the Little Big Horn massacre.

reinforcements on foot were at least a day distant. Custer knew the situation was dangerous. Intelligence told him the enemy's forces were very large. Fresh animal droppings told him he was closing in on his prey.

The mystery remains. Given all the available intelligence, why did Custer fight? The points of view expressed by various commentators vary greatly.

Why Did Custer Fight?

Gen. Hugh L. Scott wrote that Custer had not originally wanted to attack on his own. He had intended, wrote Scott, "to hide on the divide and to attack at daylight of the twenty-sixth of June but he had a right to feel that he had been discovered by Indians." Scott believed Custer had no choice but to fight.

Not so, writes David Nevin. He believes that Custer intended to fight regardless of difficulties. Custer wanted a victory, achieved on his own, without Terry and perhaps without Reno or Benteen. With such a victory, "Custer expected to regain some of the national fame he had won during the Civil War."

Nevin points out that, contrary to General Sherman's specific orders, Custer took along a reporter, Mark Kellogg, to send back stories of his heroism. Mark Kellogg worked for the *New York Herald*, whose editor, James Gordon Bennett, was Custer's friend. Bennett wielded a good deal of political influence nationally. He did not want Grant to win a third term in office. The nation was looking for a new hero. It sent along a reporter to cover the Expedition of 1876. On the hills overlooking the Little Big Horn River, Mark Kellogg paid for Custer's vanity with his life.

Historian Van de Water tries to solve the mystery with yet another explanation of why Custer ignored military intelligence available to him. He

Mark Kellogg, the young reporter for the *New York Herald*, who accompanied Custer to his death.

believes that Custer regretted the difficulties he had caused his former Civil War Commander, General Grant, through revelations concerning Orvil Grant's schemes. Being a good and loyal soldier, "Custer tried to make up with President Grant through a victory over the Indians."

If this is the case, it supports David Nevin's view that Custer "considered the presence of so many Indians the greatest luck of all." He could win a great victory against overwhelming odds. Indeed, Nevin thought Custer was a "sharp-eyed huntsman" who could "see every sign and grasp its meaning." The meaning of the opportunity on June 25, 1876, was stunning.

What Custer saw surely would have terrified a less certain or a less obsessed individual. What could have driven Custer to fight when there was still time to reevaluate and to await reinforcements?

Custer for President?

President Grant was unpopular. The Democrats were looking for a colorful, potential presidential candidate who would win the hearts of voters. David Humphrey Miller reports the words of Custer to his scouts in the last moments before the battle. "If we beat the Sioux, I will be President of the United States, the great father. If you Arakaras do as I tell you and kill Sioux for me and capture many Sioux ponies, I will take care of you all when I come to peace."

Is this then the use to which Custer put the military intelligence which had come to his hands? Have we at last arrived at the solution of the long-debated mystery? You must evaluate the opposing viewpoints presented here and arrive at your own conclusions.

Epilogue

Why Did Custer Die?

We will never know what went through Custer's mind as he wheeled his excited horses and men away from Reno's offensive, raced downriver, turned, and then suddenly saw before his tiny force of 232 men the assembled might of the Sioux nation—and attacked! The bizarre events and the unexpected outcome and the horrible results have baffled millions of Custer enthusiasts for over a hundred years.

Perhaps in the final analysis there is no mystery at all. Perhaps what took place along the banks of the Little Big Horn River was simply the final act of a great gamble and a great human tragedy. All or nothing. The presidency of the United States or martyrdom. This is not the first time a man has pitted himself against the fates—and lost.

George Armstrong Custer, courageous hero or ambitious fool?

For Further Exploration

Robert J. Casey, *The Black Hills and Their Incredible Characters*. Indianapolis: The Bobbs-Merrill Company, 1934.

Elizabeth Custer, *Boots and Saddles*. Laguna Beach, CA: Buccaneer Books, reprint of 1902 edition, 1977.

Paul and Dorothy Gable, *Custer's Last Battle*. New York: Pantheon Books, 1969.

W. A. Graham, *The Custer Myth*. Lincoln, NE: University of Nebraska Press, 1986.

Charles Hofling, *Custer and the Little Big Horn: A Psychobiographical Inquiry*. Detroit, MI: Wayne State University Press, 1986.

Charles Kuhlman, *Did Custer Disobey Orders?* Detroit, MI: Wayne State University Press, 1981.

William S. McFeely, *Grant: A Biography*. New York: W. W. Norton & Co., 1982.

David H. Miller, *Custer's Fall: The Indian Side of the Story*. Lincoln, NE: University of Nebraska Press, 1985.

David Nevin, *The Old West: The Soldiers*. New York: Time-Life Books, Inc., 1974.

Edgar I. Stewart, *Custer's Luck*. Norman, OK: University of Oklahoma Press, 1985.

Robert M. Utley, *Custer and the Great Controversy*. Los Angeles: Westernlore Press, 1962.

Robert M. Utley, *The Indian Frontier of the American West 1846-1890*. Albuquerque: University of New Mexico Press, 1984.

Frederic F. Van de Water, *Glory-Hunter: A Life of General Custer*. Lincoln, NE: University of Nebraska Press, 1988.

Stanley Vestal, *Sitting Bull*. Norman, OK: University of Oklahoma Press, 1980.

Frederick Whittaker, *A Popular Life of General George A. Custer*. New York: Sheldon & Company, 1876.

Charles A. Windolph, as told to Frazier and Robert Hunt, *I Fought with Custer*. Lincoln, NE: University of Nebraska Press, 1987.

Index

Picture Credits

Mary Ahrndt, 10, 11, 21, 40, 57

The Bettman Archive, 9, 17, 24, 28, 34, 105

Custer Battlefield National Monument, 12, 18, 20, 22, 26, 32, 37, 38, 43, 46, 49, 60, 63, 73, 78, 79, 81, 89, 100, 101, 102

Denver Public Library Western Collection, 82

The Granger Collection, 13, 29, 31, 74, 75, 84, 86

Amy Johnson, 39, 42, 53, 55, 59, 65, 77, 80, 85

Alfred Jacob Miller, National Archives of Canada, Print # C-440, 19

Minnesota Historical Society, 56, 67, 91, 94, 96

South Dakota State Historical Society, 45, 54, 62

From *Wind on the Buffalo Grass,* edited by Leslie Tillett (New York: Thomas Y. Crowel Company, 1976). Reprinted courtesy of Leslie Tillett, 14, 61, 71, 76

U.S. Military Academy, West Point, New York, 48, 68

Villa Louis, Prairie du Chien, Wisconsin, 98

About the Author

Deborah Yellin Bachrach was born and raised in New York City where she received her undergraduate education. She earned a Ph.D. in history from the University of Minnesota. Dr. Bachrach has taught at the University of Minnesota as well as St. Francis College, Joliet, Illinois, and Queens College, the City University of New York. In addition, she has worked for many years in the fields of medical research and public policy development.

Dr. Bachrach loves a good mystery but she finds that truth is often far more intriguing than fiction. *Custer's Last Stand* is her second book in the Great Mysteries series.